English
Competence
Handbook.

W9-AHE-773

THIRD EDITION

English Competence Handbook

Paul Kalkstein   Thomas J. Regan   K. Kelly Wise

Phillips Academy   Andover, Massachusetts

THE CARDEN REDWOOD SCHOOL
4500 REDWOOD ROAD
OAKLAND, CALIFORNIA 94619
Tel. 482-1160

Independent School Press

Wellesley Hills, Massachusetts

For permission to reprint copyrighted material, grateful acknowledgement is made to the following publishers and authors:

Dodd, Mead & Co., Inc. From *James Van DerZee: The Picture Takin' Man* by James Haskins, © 1979.

Alfred A. Knopf, Inc. From "Upright Carpentry" by John Updike from his *Assorted Prose*, © 1965, originally in *The New Yorker*, 10 May 1958.

The New York Times. From "The Ox-Bow Incident" review by Bosley Crowther, 10 May 1943, © 1943 by The New York Times Company. Reprinted by permission. From the editorial "Russification," 6 July 1972, © 1972 by The New York Times Company. Reprinted by permission. From "Cog Without a Wheel" by Adele Foy, 21 July 1980, © 1980 by The New York Times Company. Reprinted by permission. From "Books of the Times" by John Leonard, 21 July 1980, © 1980 by The New York Times Company. Reprinted by permission.

The New Yorker. For the obituary of Paul Desmond in "The Talk of the Town," 20 June 1977. Copyright © 1977 by The New Yorker Magazine, Inc. Reprinted by permission.

The Saturday Review Magazine Corp. From "Out-of-Sight Seeing" by John Mariani in *Saturday Review*, 22 July 1978. Copyright © 1978 by *Saturday Review*. All rights reserved. Reprinted by permission.

TIME Magazine. From "The Haunted Man" by Robert Hughes, 31 July 1972. Reprinted by permission from TIME, The Weekly Newsmagazine; Copyright Time Inc. 1972.

Cover photograph © Anthony Barboza

Copyright © 1973, 1974, 1976, 1981 by Paul Kalkstein, Thomas J. Regan and K. Kelly Wise.

All rights reserved. No part of this publication may be reproduced or transmitted in any form or by any means, electronic or mechanical, including photocopy, recording, or any information storage or retrieval system, without permission in writing from the publisher.

Printed in the United States of America.

838485
0-88334-143-3   34567890

Acknowledgements

For their initial backing of a summer project that eventually produced Andover's English Competence Program and this text, we are indebted to The Trustees of Phillips Academy and particularly to the generous support of its headmaster, Theodore R. Sizer. We also wish to thank the staff of The Independent School Press for its patience and cooperation. We owe a debt of thanks as well to our colleagues in the English Department, who have offered positive support and congenial criticism. Finally, we would be remiss if we failed to acknowledge Marnie, Gerri, and Sybil, our wives, who have humored us through the months and years of drafts and revisions.

Contents

Introduction

Competence in writing, or the ability to communicate clearly and convincingly to an audience, comes through hard work; this book is designed to help make that work fruitful. The *English Competence Handbook* provides definitions of important basic principles of sound writing. It begins with the sentence, moves to the paragraph, and aids you to build structures to work out the proofs of longer compositions. It supplies models of specific methods you can use to write more clearly and communicate more convincingly. When you have mastered these fundamental methods of competence, you should go beyond them to create your own style and your own structures, structures uniquely fitted to the ideas you wish to convey.

The *Handbook* contains many assignments for use in a course that emphasizes writing. The authors hope that you will particularly enjoy, and benefit from, the many photographs in the text. The assignments based on these photographs are grouped at the back of the book because we do not at all wish to suggest that the photographs can be limited in force or meaning. No formal art education is required to engage the photographs, nor to create with and from them vivid sentences, paragraphs, and compositions. They should help you produce writing that is fresh and fascinating as well as competent.

Knowledge of a few basic grammatical terms is helpful as you use the first part of the book. Presentations and exercises in the early pages assume that you are familiar with the parts of speech and with phrases and clauses. But the *Handbook* is not by any means a grammar text. Its "recipes" for good writing are stated in plain language, and they should help you become a more competent, effective writer.

English Competence Handbook.

I.
The Sentence

Types of Sentences

Coordination and Subordination

Structure and Idea

Rhetorical Patterns

A. New City, New York, 1971   **Arno Rafael Minkkinen**

Types of Sentences

By their structure, sentences fall into four classifications:

1. **Simple sentence:** one main clause and no subordinate clauses.

   Squeaking all the way, the squirrel disappeared in the trees.

   I trudged off for the Dean's Office, resigned to my fate.

2. **Compound sentence:** at least two main clauses and no subordinate clauses.

   It was his turn at bat, and he struck out.

   Today's menu is chili and corn bread; tomorrow's is cold cuts and potato salad.

3. **Complex sentence:** one main clause and at least one subordinate clause.

   Although his stomach rumbled and complained, he continued to eat.

   Your jacket — the leather one which you like — has been stolen.

4. **Compound-Complex sentence:** two or more main clauses and at least one subordinate clause.

   His hunch that the infection might spread over his body was confirmed; when he awoke the next day, he was covered with a rash and hives.

   Although the critics had raved about the book, Edward found it a drag; he had promised a friend that he would finish it, but guiltily he reneged on that promise.

B. Untitled, 1977   **Ann Mandelbaum**

Coordination and Subordination

The conjunction *and* is a coordinate conjunction — that is, it is meant to connect two grammatically equal constructions:

(single words) Alvin and Belinda . . .

(prepositional phrases) Alvin ran into the house and up the stairs.

(subordinate clauses) When Belinda had arrived and while the music was still playing, we decided to . . .

(main clauses) I detest fried food and I'll tell you why.

The logic of coordination asserts that two constructions joined by a coordinate conjunction are of equal importance. These constructions should relate in some way. In an essay you might wish to mention your fondness for your grandmother and also your fear of heights. Although these two ideas may be of equal importance, they do not easily relate and would seem absurd if joined by a conjunction. "I have always been fond of my grandmother and I have a fear of heights."

It is also illogical to join with *and* two ideas that are related but are of unequal importance.

"Alvin is not driving to Albany today and his car has a flat tire."

Most likely the two clauses are of unequal importance; one clause should be subordinated to the other. If addressed to Alvin's garage mechanic, the statement should place emphasis on the flat tire, and the idea of driving to Albany should be relegated to a subordinate clause. But if the statement is addressed to someone needing a ride to Albany, its emphasis should be reversed.

(to the mechanic) "Alvin's car is in such bad shape that he can't go to Albany today." (less important idea becomes a result clause — but see the final comments to this section)

(to the prospective passenger) "Alvin is not driving to Albany today because his car has a flat tire." (less important idea becomes a cause clause)

Other coordinate conjunctions are *but, for, yet, or, nor. And,* the easiest to use, has the least meaning. It connects elements of a sentence; it does not state relationships or designate order. Before using a coordinate conjunction, determine the relationship between the elements of your sentence; then choose the conjunction to express that relationship or another grammatical device to do the job.

One warning about coordination: it can be used to a fault. As they begin to conceptualize, children are often guilty of excessive coordination. Their stories ramble on and on, clause after clause connected by conjunctions. The mind as well as the ear needs phrases, clauses, ideas categorized for it. Through subordination and the use of transitions, you can help the reader to understand your ideas. Major points will appear in main clauses, perhaps even in simple declarative sentences; minor points and modifiers will be subordinated.

Proper subordination is vital to effective prose. Although the subordinate clause is probably the most familiar device for subordination, remember that the possible variations are numerous: the main clause that must be subordinated can be altered to a prepositional phrase, a verbal, a simple adjective, an appositive — or it may be involved in a complete revision of the sentence. For example:

> "Alvin isn't driving to Albany today because of a flat tire." (a prepositional phrase and only one clause)

> "Alvin's flat tire prevents him from driving to Albany today." (revision, and only one clause)

But when we have finished our study of the logic of subordination, we are left with an irony: occasionally the most important idea in a sentence occurs properly in a subordinate clause, but achieves its effect by some other means, like being at the end (the climactic position) of the sentence. One can argue, for instance, that the result clause addressed to the mechanic contains the key idea:

> Alvin's car is in *such* bad shape *that he can't go to Albany today.*

And consider the following:

> He is the man *who attacked the policeman.* (relative clause)

> I think *that Stephen ought to see a doctor about his knee injury.* (noun clause)

Exercises

A. Underline and identify each subordinate clause below:

1. One need not read every article or preposition, although the slow reader thinks otherwise.
2. This is how I would describe the incident.
3. Wherever you lead, I will follow.
4. Be alert for the thesis statement as you are reading.
5. Romanticism arose in rebellion against the ideals of reason and rational form which had governed taste in the late seventeenth and eighteenth centuries.

B. Underline and identify each verbal phrase below:

1. I always wanted to go to Africa.
2. The superfluous shawl, dangling from her arm, did not protect her from the hot sun.
3. Having defeated the Black Knight, Lancelot returned to the Round Table.
4. Knowing the material is the first step towards an honor grade.
5. After raking the leaves, the old gardener left the millionaire's house and went to his next job.

C. Indicate sentence type: simple, complex, compound, compound-complex.

1. To assert your independence, you should boycott the meeting.
2. I have always known that she was fond of me; what I didn't know was that she regarded me as a spiritual brother.
3. After we rehearsed the play for five hours, we went to a local diner, where we had delicious pastrami sandwiches.
4. Evan is sometimes quite aloof; I can't figure it out — his brother and sister are both open and friendly.
5. Deceit is characteristic of his nature, unfortunately, and he regrets this.
6. The editorial today was inflammatory, structured upon hateful assumptions and allegations.
7. Any one of us could help, if you would only ask.
8. "Running for office places one in difficult positions," he said; "and often I find myself biting my lip, knowing I must suppress what comes to mind."

9. She is the kind of selfless being whom one encounters rarely these days.

10. A sense of humor, an interest in others, a willingness to accept criticism — these personal traits are Ralph's.

D. Test for effective coordination and subordination. Be prepared to discuss these sentences in class.

1. "The blunder is clearly mine," he said; and dropping his eyes, he shambled off.

2. Sylvia, who sleeps in the bunk beside mine, has a radio that she turns on quite early each morning.

3. We went swimming, but I locked the key in the car and my date was furious because she knew we would be late getting home.

4. The ball bounced off the rim and the gun sounded; we had lost the game.

5. Any proxy given may be revoked by a stockholder at any time before it is voted by filing with the secretary a notice in writing revoking it, or by executing a proxy bearing a later date.

6. Innis courteously refused, but Harter sought support among his friends, persuading several of them to underwrite their magazine.

7. Sarah reached for her bag and she hissed as she rose: "You presume too much and with your conceit you will always presume too much."

8. "My contention is this." He paused. "If people continue to kill one another as they are, the world will only get worse, and since there are more people than ever before and the instruments of murder are ever more available, our civilization is doomed."

Structure and Idea

Through parallelism, subordination, coordination, and the use of correlatives, you can help the reader understand your ideas. As you write, you are continually making decisions, however subconsciously, about the structure of your sentences. There are times when you will be best served by lining up your ideas in neat clauses and tacking them together, one after another, with semicolons. There are other times when you will need a contrast in structure, and therefore you will begin with a word like *although*. Still other times correlatives, such as *not only . . . but also*, will provide the form in which to cast your ideas.

Other correlative pairs include

both . . . and . . .

as . . . as . . .

neither . . . nor . . .

either . . . or . . .

whether . . . or . . .

C. New York City, 1963   Lee Friedlander

Rhetorical Patterns

Word order, emphasis, balance, subordination, rhythm — all these belong to rhetoric. A sentence may be more effective because the writer places a word or a phrase at its end; or he balances a construction; or he establishes a contrast.

Our language is predicated upon the natural structure of the simple declarative sentence: subject, verb, object. Yet our ears and minds demand variety. When we repeat the same structure over and over, we mock ourselves, as a sing-song rime mocks itself. Any good writer knows this. His writing is interesting not only because of its substance and theme but also because of its rhetoric (the structure and liveliness of its language).

The successful writer can use techniques of structure to enliven his prose. These techniques he acquires through his own good instincts as well as through the example of classical writers. He senses when these techniques should be used; he knows that they can dull his effect if they are ill-timed or overworked.

To open a sentence with a word such as *that* or *if* followed by a noun will force him into a new pattern. Similarly, he may begin with an infinitive or a gerund and vary his syntax. Other rhetorical patterns are more classical: inversion, periodic sentence, balanced sentence, antithesis, repetition for effect.

Inversion (a reversal of the normal order of a sentence):

> On November 6, 1817, died the Princess Charlotte, only child of the Prince Regent, and heir to the crown of England. (Lytton Strachey, *Queen Victoria*)

> Out of the hills, through the canyons, down into the deserted town galloped the Dalton brothers.

Periodic Sentence (main idea at the end of the sentence):

> If we are to quiet the nation's fears, if we are to overcome the many problems that lie ahead, if we are to build a secure and prosperous future, right now we must, with all our will, strive for unity.

> It was obvious now that he had always, passionately, lied.

Balanced Sentence (equal ideas in parallel structure):

> Yesterday many stood in the rain to pray with the Pope; today some of those people may have colds and couldn't care less.

> What we need is rekindled faith in our cause; what we need is renewed energy; what we need is plain hard work.

Antithesis (parallel structure to contrast opposing ideas):

I am familiar with Sterne's face, but have never seen its changing expressions, have taken the measure of his form, but never observed his gestures, have read his words, but never heard his intonations. (Arthur H. Cash, *Laurence Sterne, the Early and Middle Years*)

The ubiquitous television may be our enemy, if we turn to it without regard for content; or it may be our friend, if we select wisely what we view.

Repetition of a word, phrase, or clause:

He shared the conviction of the angry mob, a conviction worthy of respect.

Wandering down bleak streets at dusk, skulking in murky alleys after dark, strutting at noon along teeming sidewalks, these young men are desperate about their futures — and about their nows.

We shall not flag or fail. We shall fight in France, we shall fight on the seas and oceans, we shall fight with growing confidence and growing strength in the air, we shall defend our island, whatever the cost may be, we shall fight on the beaches, we shall fight on the landing grounds, we shall fight in the fields and in the streets, we shall fight in the hills; we shall never surrender. (Winston Churchill, Speech before House of Commons)

Some other sentence constructions:

Gerund opener:

Loving is what plays one least false. (Henry James, *The Ambassadors*)

Infinitive opener:

To sacrifice for the good of others is a Christian ideal.

A, B, C series with dash:

Integrity, wholesomeness, cordiality — in Maria all three may be found in abundance.

That construction:

That duplicity is a temptation for him seems more and more apparent.

Of construction:

Of the expense for her birthday party, she was most conscious.

Exercises

A. Complete the sentences as indicated below:

  1. Antithesis:

     For days it had not rained, but . . . (complete the sentence)

     Albert is open, friendly, with a generous nature; his friend Silas
     . . . (complete the sentence)

  2. Inversion:

     Smiling between delighted gulps, Gretta slaked her thirst with
     minty iced tea. (invert the construction)

  3. Noun clause as subject:

     That insincerity is a fault . . . (complete the sentence)

  4. Balanced Sentence, Using Phrases:

     . . . concerned about . . . concerned about . . . (create a sentence
     using these phrases)

  5. Balanced Sentence, Using Clauses:

     It was critical that . . .; it was critical that . . . (create a sentence
     that employs this repetition)

  6. Periodic Sentence:

     Alyson, a staunch nationalist, is most troubled by the proposed
     conditional amnesty, a proposal that seems to her immoral. (con-
     vert this sentence into a periodic sentence)

  7. Repetition of a Word:

     Integrity . . . integrity (create a sentence that employs this repeti-
     tion)

B. What two rhetorical patterns are prominent in this paragraph
   from Samuel Johnson's "Life of Richard Savage"? Use at least
   one of these patterns in a paragraph of your own about a person
   you know well.

   In this manner were passed those days and those nights which nature
   had enabled him to have employed in elevated speculations, useful
   studies, or pleasing conversations. On a bulk, in a cellar, or in a glass-
   house, among thieves and beggars, was to be found the author of
   "The Wanderer," the man of exalted sentiments, extensive views, and

curious observations; the man whose remarks on life might have assisted the statesman, whose ideas of virtue might have enlightened the moralist, whose eloquence might have influenced senates, and whose delicacy might have polished courts.

C. What rhetorical patterns dominate this paragraph from Ralph Waldo Emerson's "Self-Reliance"? Create five sentences of your own, using at least two patterns you have identified in Emerson's paragraph.

The civilized man has built a coach, but has lost the use of his feet. He is supported on crutches, but lacks so much support of muscle. He has a fine Geneva watch, but he fails of the skill to tell the hour by the sun. A Greenwich nautical almanac he has, and so being sure of the information when he wants it, the man in the street does not know a star in the sky. The solstice he does not observe; the equinox he knows as little; and the whole bright calendar of the year is without a dial in his mind. His notebooks impair his memory; his libraries overload his wit; the insurance office increases the number of accidents; and it may be a question whether machinery does not encumber; whether we have not lost by refinement some energy, by a Christianity entrenched in establishments and forms, some vigor of wild virtue. For every Stoic was a Stoic; but in Christendom where is the Christian?

D. Discuss the effect of the following sentences. Create a new structure for each, preserving the ideas in the original.

One ever feels his twoness — an American, a Negro; two souls, two thoughts; two unreconciled strivings, two warring ideals in one dark body. (W.E.B. DuBois, *The Souls of Black Folk*)

To argue that we should support the present Gun Control Law is to place inordinate faith in the rationality and good will of modern man, a creature often hell-bent upon the destruction of himself and others.

I tried to break the spell — the heavy, mute spell of the wilderness — that seemed to draw him to its pitiless breast by the awakening of forgotten and brutal instincts, by the memory of gratified and monstrous passions. (Joseph Conrad, *Heart of Darkness*)

Urbane, gregarious, fickle, a man who acts upon clever hunches about his competitors, the oil magnate has slowly amassed a considerable fortune.

His life was like a book broken in the back, which falls into two parts. (Van Wyck Brooks, *John Addington Symonds*)

D. Terra Firma, 1974   **Bobbi Carrey**

For the first time they would be alone together indoors, and they would sit there, one on each side of the stove, like a married couple, he in his stocking feet and smoking his pipe, she laughing and talking in that funny way she had, which was always as new to him as if he had never heard her before. (Edith Wharton, *Ethan Frome*)

If we had a keen vision and feeling of all ordinary human life, it would be like hearing the grass grow, and the squirrel's heart beat, and we should die of that roar which lies on the other side of silence. (George Eliot, *Middlemarch*)

E. Explain the differences in emphasis and effect in the pairs of sentences below.

1. Mildred lacks confidence in her own talent; last night when she held up that vase of flowers she had arranged, her hands fluttered like birds.

   That Mildred was far from confident about the success of her flower arrangement could be detected by her trembling hands when she held up the vase to the audience.

2. I could hear the siren wailing in the distance; help would soon arrive.

   In the distance wailed a siren — help was on its way.

3. But at that moment the sail swung slowly round, filled slowly out, the boat seemed to shake herself, and then to move off half conscious in her sleep, and then she woke and shot through the waves. (Virginia Woolf, *To The Lighthouse*)

   We drifted slowly, the sail limp, and then a sudden spurt of wind caught us and we cut through the waves.

4. Without imagination our souls grow weary and life seems a dismantled circus.

   Clearly it is imagination that colors existence, makes of our dull days something romantic, elusive, and grand.

5. Achievement measured by his own personally high standards, that was what he counted as success.

   He judged success by measuring up to his own high standards.

6. The garden was ready — the earth had been plowed and fertilized.

   The garden had been carefully tilled; manure had been shoveled into the rows; the earth lay ready to plant.

F. Repair the following sentences. Employ more descriptive language. Avoid vagueness, imprecision, and weak subordination.

1. The first time I saw her she had on those long earrings that I've seen actresses wear and jeans I know came from an attic, which is what she usually wore.

2. Calmly and systematically, the fire warden ordered that we open all doors and windows enabling the steam gushing through the standing radiator to escape.

3. The day progressed in its slow, dull way until a voice from afar was heard calling for help.

4. Harry Talbert, the coach, scratched his chin as he thought, slowly watching his skaters on the ice then on the bench, to insure himself he had the correct group of talent playing these all-important minutes.

5. Several minutes later all of my clothing and goods had been hauled up to join me in my quarters, and I sprawled on my bed and waited to meet my roommate.

6. Each morning before daylight begins he lifts his body heavily from the bed and leaves his humble hut to kneel by the active stream; here, it is his wish to honor the gods and ask them for a lot of animals and some rain for the fields.

7. My friend does very good in school — to show you where her head is at, she likes chemistry and history.

8. An egret moves slowly, ever so quietly, through the wet mud that stinks so, seeking food, while a seagull takes all this in from a pier and cleans a supper of garbage and mussels from his face.

9. The singing of the wren, a friendly sound, was interrupted by the noise of a squirrel, as it called and talked to a mate nearby in an old oak tree.

10. An engine's headlight drifted through the darkness and illuminated the angry protestors' activity.

E. Newark, New Jersey, 1962   **Lee Friedlander**

II.
The Paragraph

Paragraph Elements

Transitions

Methods of Paragraph Development

The Topic Sentence

The topic sentence is the keystone of the paragraph. It may be an explicit statement of the central idea or a generalization which in cludes all of the ideas in the paragraph. Although it is most common to place the topic sentence at the beginning of the paragraph, it may come in the middle or — for reasons of emphasis — at the end. (In some instances the topic idea will not be stated; instead, it will merely be implied.) You should take great care in constructing the topic sentence, for it is important in producing concrete and effective prose.

The same considerations of word choice, structure, and subordination which are important in the sentence are central to paragraph development. Whereas a sentence states a single idea, a paragraph develops a central idea, providing a broader or deeper view. Some of the basic elements of effective paragraphs are unity, coherence, emphasis, clarity, and concreteness.

This paragraph from *Lacrosse Fundamentals* by G. H. Evans and R. Anderson shows the use of a strong, controlling topic sentence. It is unified and coherent as well.

> Frequently spectators uninitiated in lacrosse gain the impression that the contest is rough since players are "swinging sticks at each other," but anyone who has played will quickly assure them that is far from true. The play is always wide open; and while there is frequent contact, serious lacrosse injuries are quite rare. Relatively little contact is generally the rule when skilled opponents meet. The stick itself looks like a dangerous weapon, but in reality, if the defensive player is skilled, his checks with the crosse are legal and non-injurious. Wild swinging is illegal, as is slashing or hitting other than on the opponent's stick or gloves. Occasionally blows are caught on the arms, but these are softened by the player's arm pads and do little damage.

Unity

A unified piece of writing has a single central idea, a single dominant effect, or both. All of the details included must pertain to that idea or effect; no irrelevant material may be included. The single idea or effect may be simple (as in a sentence or a paragraph) or complex (as in an essay or a story). Unity is an outgrowth of good organization and development. Crisp sentences, meaningful transitions, paragraphs focused by strong topic sentences, consistency of tenses — all are used to create unity.

This paragraph about Henry II of England, in Joseph B. Strayer's *Western Europe in the Middle Ages*, is well unified. All of the sentences bear directly on the central idea, and a frame structure, recapitulating the first idea in the last sentence, helps to hold the paragraph together.

> At the same time that Henry was increasing the functions of the circuit judges, he was introducing the use of the jury. The idea was an old one — it went back at least to the Carolingian kings — but it had never been extensively used before. The jury was a device for giving a ruler authentic information; Maitland defined it as "a body of neighbors summoned by a public officer to give upon oath a true answer to a question." Frankish kings had used it to determine boundaries of royal estates, and William the Conqueror had obtained a description of all English landholdings — the famous Domesday survey — by the testimony of jurors in every township. The jury had also been used to settle disputes between the great landholders; it gave the king the facts and so enabled him to decide the case without suspicion of favoritism. But it had been used only sparingly until the time of Henry II; no subject had a right to demand a jury and no general class of lawsuits was regularly settled by jury verdicts.

Coherence

A coherent piece of writing is literally one that "sticks together." Parts of a paragraph or composition must be related to each other as well as to the whole, and they must follow each other logically and clearly. Word must follow word; clause follow clause; sentence, sentence; and paragraph, paragraph. Grammatical structure and diction (word choice) must be consistent to ensure coherence.

The careful choice of the appropriate paragraph development technique will aid in achieving coherence. Paragraphs ordered by space, time, classification, or other schemes are likely to be coherent, especially if you employ a strong topic sentence. For coherence in a sentence or subordinate clause, be sure that your pronoun references are clear, that modifiers are placed beside the words they modify, and that conjunctions are used correctly.

Lawrence A. Cremin, in *The Transformation of the School*, discusses reform movements in American secondary education. Note the unity and coherence of the paragraph below: the topic sentence links the paragraph to the one preceding it; Cremin uses several transitional devices to make the sentences flow smoothly; ideas proceed in a logical order.

> Just as diversity characterized the private progressive schools of the interbellum era, so diversity marked the vast number of public-school experiments. The twenties and thirties were an age of reform in American education, as thousands of local districts adopted one or another of the elements in the progressive program. As might be expected, the movement proceeded at a vastly uneven pace, varying from region to region and from state to state. And as in earlier times, different aspects of progressivism were taken up by different communities, depending on circumstances and clientele. It would be pointless to try to catalogue this plethora of reform, since the job has already been done in some detail by the sundry publications of the National Society for the Study of Education and the Society for Curriculum Study. But perhaps a few notable examples will suffice.

Emphasis

Some ideas are more important than others. A good writer helps the reader to recognize the more important ideas or details in his composition by placing emphasis on them. Effective emphasis in the sentence results from proper subordination (lesser details in subordinate clauses), accurate diction, and word order. In a paragraph, placement of the central idea, the topic sentence, is crucial; generally, it will appear at the beginning or at the end of the paragraph. Another consideration that will strengthen emphasis within a paragraph is syntax (sentence structure). Periodic sentences, in which basic grammatical structure and meaning are not complete until the end of the sentence, are more emphatic than loose sentences. Emphasis in a longer composition results from careful placement of all of the central ideas and topic sentences, and variety of syntax. For example, a short, striking paragraph at the beginning or end of a composition might provide an emphatic setting for the central idea.

In this excerpt from Kenneth Eble's *A Perfect Education*, note the effect of the simple declarative sentences which build to the topic sentence. The paragraph concludes with a sudden and skillful shift in emphasis.

> By such means we come to see the world feelingly and not alone. Our joys are more intense for being shared. Our sorrows are less destructive for our knowing of universal sorrows. Our pride is chastened by an awareness of our betters. Our fears of death fade before the commonness of the occurrence. All humanity argues against our marching blindly toward death. Education, above all, gives value to life. The more we see on the way, the more we feel, the more we ponder over our journey, the more we ask of education, and the more it can give.

Clarity

If there is confusion in your mind about the subject you are dealing with, you are not likely to clarify it for the reader. Once you have come to a clear understanding of the subject, you must find accurate words to convey your meaning and an appropriate structure to fit your subject.

Often clarity is achieved through conciseness: creating sentences and paragraphs that are precise, with all ambiguity and wordiness pruned from them. Clarity is also achieved through structure. For the sentence, this often means good use of parallel structure, so that elements of an idea or statement are easy to grasp. Correlatives, coordinate conjunctions, rhetorical patterns (such as periodic or balanced sentences and antithesis) — all these can aid through structure to enhance clarity.

The most important tool for clarity is diction. Noun phrases and verbs demand special attention. Effective diction depends upon noun phrases to serve a number of purposes: they define, they delineate, and they discriminate among classifiable and subtle points. It is a simple task to identify spots in a prose passage that lack the necessary clarity and assertion of noun phrases, for these spots often contain skeins of tiny words — adjectives, adverbs, articles, and prepositions. ("She was a proud young lady who refused to lie and whose words could be understood without exaggeration" is a construction that could be reduced in length and strengthened by using the word *integrity*.) Of equal importance, effective diction requires verbs of action, charged with color and feeling. (*Abandon* or *forsake* rather than *drop*; *nurtures* rather than *helps*; *discloses* rather than *presents*.)

Concreteness

A topic sentence is a generalization. If a reader is to grasp the idea or ideas in the sentence clearly, the rest of the paragraph must provide specific details to support and illustrate the generalization. The statement "Fish abound in the waters off Balagua" is general. To make that statement concrete to the reader, the writer should develop the paragraph with details like "Piranhas prey around the rocks at low tide," and "Sand sharks sport near the reefs off the town jetty." Note the verbs in those statements. They are strong, cast in the active voice. Beware of overworking the verb *to be;* seek lively, descriptive verbs for your writing.

Selection of precise and vivid details enlivens the following paragraph from Frederick Lewis Allen's *Only Yesterday.* The paragraph describes the prelude to the stock market crash of 1929.

> All the same, it had been a frightful day. At seven o'clock that night the tickers in a thousand brokers' offices were still chattering; not till after 7:08 did they finally record the last sale made on the floor at three o'clock. The volume of trading had set a new record — 12,894,650 shares. ("The time may come when we shall see a five-million-share day," the wise men of the Street had been saying twenty months before!) Incredible rumors had spread wildly during the early afternoon — that eleven speculators had committed suicide, that the Buffalo and Chicago exchanges had been closed, that troops were guarding the New York Stock Exchange against an angry mob. The country had known the bitter taste of panic. And although the bankers' pool had prevented for the moment an utter collapse, there was no gainsaying the fact that the economic structure had cracked wide open.

Exercises

A. Construct paragraphs from each of the following topic sentences. Notice how the topic sentence controls or dictates the development of the paragraph.

1. Paper clips are useful for more than holding papers together.
2. Junk food is more fattening than home-prepared meals.
3. Dancing requires not only agility, but stamina as well.

B. Although the following paragraph from Hamlin Garland's *A Son of the Middle Border* lacks a definite topic sentence, it is well unified. State in a sentence the central, unifying idea in the paragraph. Then explain in a sentence or two how Garland achieves coherence in the paragraph.

As harvest came on he took command in the field, for most of the harvest help that year were rough, hardy wanderers from the south, nomads who had followed the line of ripening wheat from Missouri northward, and were not the most profitable companions for boys of fifteen. They reached our neighborhood in July, arriving like a flight of alien unclean birds, and vanished into the north in September as mysteriously as they had appeared. A few of them had been soldiers, others were the errant sons of the poor farmers, and rough mechanics of older States, migrating for the adventure of it. One of them gave his name as "Harry Lee," others were known by such names as "Big Ed" or "Shorty." Some carried valises, others had nothing but small bundles containing a clean shirt and a few socks.

C. Identify the topic sentence in each of the following paragraphs. If it is not accurate and clear, rewrite it. Then examine each of the paragraphs for unity, coherence, clarity, concreteness, and conciseness. Find at least three examples of vague, or wordy, or poorly-structured phrases; improve each example.

1. Plywood is one of the most useful building materials that can be found today. Manufactured either for indoor or outdoor exposure, it can be bought in different sizes, thicknesses, and finishes. The thin sheets of wood glued together to make up plywood come from the lower parts of softwood trees. A large lathe steel blade is used to cut the log into various veneers. These then are dried, trimmed, run through a glue spreader, and laid up to be pressed into panels.

2. I have always liked the protagonist of Ayn Rand's novel, *The Fountainhead*. Howard Roark is dynamic and he is also the central motivator of the plot. What appeals to me is his independence; nobody is going to push him around. His architectural designs are originals. Like his character, his buildings are sturdy, functional, without ambiguity; they are built out of human need and they have neither excess nor frills to them. He is an example to all — never compromise.

3. For a little basic botany and a lot of fun, apartment gardeners for years have sown beans in Dixie cups. This technique is foolproof, and it takes little attention and is adaptable. Certainly it eliminates the fear of animals. Beans planted this way don't take up much room, and naturally they are just as delicious as those staked up on poles or grown in bushes in open-air gardens.

Transitions

Transitions can occur within a sentence, between sentences in a paragraph, and between paragraphs. They are devices that help to connect ideas, reveal relationships among various statements, distinguish conditions, point out new directions to be followed. Without transitions the flow of ideas in a composition is interrupted.

Sometimes a sentence itself is used as a transition. More commonly, phrases are used, such as the following:

Transitions	Function
similarly, in the same way	comparison
moreover, furthermore	addition, amplification
but, yet, however, on the other hand	change, exception, opposition
nevertheless, notwithstanding, still	concession
by contrast, unlike, instead	contrast
in order that, so that	purpose
for, because	explanation
although, whereas	concession, balance
for example, for instance	illustration
provided that, except that	restriction
even though, as if	qualification, uncertainty
in fact, certainly, indeed	emphasis
suddenly, as soon as, before	time
consequently, therefore	consequence
so . . . that . . .	result

THE CARDEN REDWOOD SCHOOL
4500 REDWOOD ROAD
OAKLAND, CALIFORNIA 94619
Tel. 482-1160

Exercise

Underline the transitional words and phrases in this paragraph from *Talks to Teachers* by William James. Note that not all of them occur at the beginnings of sentences.

Every school has its tone, moral and intellectual. And this tone is a mere tradition kept up by imitation, due in the first instance to the example set by teachers and by previous pupils of an aggressive and dominating type, copied by the others, and passed on from year to year, so that the new pupils take the cue almost immediately. Such a tone changes very slowly, if at all; and then always under the modifying influence of new personalities aggressive enough in character to set new patterns and not merely to copy the old. The classic example of this sort of tone is the often quoted case of Rugby under Dr. Arnold's administration. He impressed his own character as a model on the imagination of the oldest boys, who in turn were expected and required to impress theirs upon the younger set. The contagiousness of Arnold's genius was such that a Rugby man was said to be recognizable all through life by a peculiar turn of character which he acquired at school. It is obvious that psychology as such can give in this field no precepts of detail. As in so many other fields of teaching, success depends mainly on the native genius of the teacher, the sympathy, tact, and perception which enable him to seize the right moment and to set the right example.

Methods of Paragraph Development

I. Organization of Details for Description and Narration

    A. Spatial Organization

    B. Chronological Organization

II. Organization of Ideas for Exposition

    A. Example

    B. Definition

    C. Process

    D. Classification and Division

    E. Cause and Effect

    F. Comparison and Contrast

    G. Analogy

    H. Analysis

G. Untitled   **Anthony Barboza**

Paragraph Development

In order that your writing be enlightening rather than muddling to your reader, your paragraphs must be ordered. That is, they must have unity and coherence, and they should follow a method of development. Paragraph unity means that all details in the paragraph must pertain to a central idea or design. Coherence means that details and ideas follow one another in logical order, so that a reader can grasp them easily. Each topic should lend itself to at least one method of development. Some methods suit descriptive or narrative writing, others expository writing.

I. Organization of Details for Description and Narration

A. Spatial Organization

In a description, you are trying to create a mental picture for the reader. That impression will be blurred if your details occur in no particular order. To create a sharp impression, you must select your details with regard to some scheme. The reader will follow you if you arrange details from *left to right* or from *near to far*, or from *up to down*. Other schemes are possible; for instance, you might choose to describe the view from the top steps of a museum by following the curving path that leads out from the steps. The path, then, would help determine the spatial organization for your description.

The spot where you stand or sit to describe a scene is called your point of view. It should not change if the impression you create is to remain unified.

F. Scott Fitzgerald uses spatial organization in this description of the Buchanan house in *The Great Gatsby:*

> And so it happened that on a warm windy evening I drove over to East Egg to see two old friends whom I scarcely knew at all. Their house was even more elaborate than I expected, a cheerful red-and-white Georgian Colonial mansion, overlooking the bay. The lawn started at the beach and ran toward the front door for a quarter of a mile, jumping over sun-dials and brick walks and burning gardens — finally when it reached the house drifting up the side in bright vines as though from the momentum of its run. The front was broken by a line of French windows, glowing now with reflected gold and wide

open to the warm windy afternoon, and Tom Buchanan in riding clothes was standing with his legs apart on the front porch.

B. Chronological Organization

When you narrate an action as it would occur in time, you are using chronological organization. This method of paragraph development is a familiar one; we encounter it every day in the newspaper — a fire, a robbery, the town meeting. The use of transitions *(then, five minutes later, suddenly, after that)* lends a rhythm, an immediacy to the impression.

Consider the effect of chronology as the organizing principle in this paragraph from Thackeray's *Vanity Fair:*

> Half-an-hour afterwards there was a great hurry and bustle in the house. Lights went about from window to window in the lonely desolate old Hall, whereof but two or three rooms were ordinarily occupied by its owner. Presently, a boy on a pony went galloping off to Mudbury, to the Doctor's house there. And in another hour (by which fact we ascertain how carefully the excellent Mrs. Bute Crawley had always kept up an understanding with the great house), that lady in her clogs and calash, the Reverend Bute Crawley, and James Crawley her son, had walked over from the Rectory through the park, and had entered the mansion by the open hall-door.

II. Organization of Ideas for Exposition

The categories of "details" and "ideas" are not exclusive: writing about ideas may include details, and writing about details may include ideas.

Furthermore the eight types of expository paragraphs which follow are by no means the only patterns possible. Because his subject matter is often complex, defying simple structuring, a good writer uses combinations of types in his writing. As you gain experience in organizing your ideas, you should move from imitation of these eight types to the creation of your own types of paragraph development. The structure of your paragraphs should depend on your subject matter and the use you wish to make of it.

A. Example

One way to develop a paragraph is to follow the topic sentence with a number of examples which prove or illustrate the idea of that sentence. Your ideas should be arranged in some sort of order. The two most common arrangements are to begin with the most important (or most striking) example and proceed down the page with supporting details to augment the case; or to save the most telling detail until the end of the paragraph, using other details to build up to it.

Washington Irving's description of John Bull, the typical British country squire, shows development by example.

> He is given, however, to indulge his veneration for family usages, and family encumbrances, to a whimsical extent. His manor is infested by gangs of gipsies; yet he will not suffer them to be driven off, because they have infested the place time out of mind, and been regular poachers upon every generation of the family. He will scarcely permit a dry branch to be lopped from the great trees that surround the house, lest it should molest the rooks, that have bred there for centuries. Owls have taken possession of the dovecote; but they are hereditary owls, and must not be disturbed. Swallows have nearly choked up every chimney with their nests; martins build in every frieze and cornice; crows flutter about the towers, and perch on every weathercock; and old gray-headed rats may be seen in every quarter of the house, running in and out of their holes undauntedly in broad daylight. In short, John has such reverence for everything that has been long in the family, that he will not hear even of abuses being reformed, because they are good old family abuses.

Often a writer wishing to prove a certain point will state that point in his topic sentence and work out the proof in a paragraph developed by example, as Rosemary Hughes does here:

> Haydn did not 'invent' the string quartet. Music for strings in four parts was already being written throughout his adolescence and young manhood: by Italians such as Tartini, Pugnani, and the Sammartini brothers, by the splendidly progressive group of composers working in Mannheim and led by Johann Stamitz and Franz Xaver Richter, by the much-admired Florian Gassmann in Vienna.

B. Definition

Development of an idea by definition involves much more than a dictionary treatment of that idea or term. Often you will need to distinguish as you define; i.e., tell your reader both what your idea or term *is* and what it *is not*.

A formal definition requires that first you establish the class to which a term belongs and then differentiate it from others in that class. "A porringer (term) is (linking verb) a dish (class) used for eating porridge or cereal, especially by children (differentiation)."

Informal definition is often more concerned with the connotations of a word (ideas suggested by the word) than with its denotations (dictionary meaning).

You may choose to take one or more routes of definition. Some of these are size (a baseball is the size of an orange), texture or composition, use or function, example, comparison or contrast with other objects (not only by size), derivation or historical development.

Here is an informal definition paragraph by Jim Haskins:

> The forerunner of the camera, the "camera obscura," was developed in ancient times. The Latin words mean "dark room," and the first kinds were small, darkened rooms whose only light source was a single, tiny hole in one wall. The light coming through that hole would cast on the opposite wall an upside-down image of the scene outside the wall with the hole in it. It was basically a large version of the pinhole cameras that children nowadays are taught to make out of a box with a pinhole in one side.

Here is another, by Jose Torres in his biography of the boxer Muhammad Ali:

> Ali is not a great fighter in the conventional sense that Sugar Ray Robinson, Willie Pep and Joe Louis were. Each of these fighters knew every punch and every move and added some tricks to the book, that unwritten book whose teachings are passed on from gym to gym and are the nearest thing we [fighters] have to our own culture.

C. Process

If you are writing to tell someone how to do something — how to get to downtown Boston from Wellesley or how to make lobster newburg — you are writing a process essay. List your steps in chronological order and state them accurately; otherwise, you confuse your reader.

> To find a book you want, first look it up in the CARD CATALOG. There you will find a number which will show you where in the stacks (the shelves) the book is located. There are four types of cards in the card catalog: author cards, title cards, subject cards, and subject cross-reference cards. If you are writing a paper on seraphim, for instance, and you are looking for a book called *Wielders of the Flaming Sword*, by John Wyrostek, simply look up either author (Wyrostek) or title *(Wielders . . .)*. If you know of no specific book on seraphim, look up "seraphim" in the card catalog and you may find subject references. In addition, a subject cross-reference card might send you to another subject heading ("Seraphim see Angels — names and types"). If you find your book in the catalog, write down its title and number on a piece of paper, check at the entrance to the stacks for the general location of the number, and find your book in the stacks. Be sure to sign the book out at the desk.

D. Classification and Division

Classification and division are similar in that both involve placing details, things, or ideas into firm categories. The only distinction is that you classify plural subjects (like trees) into categories and you divide singular subjects (a tree) into parts. In either case, before you can analyze the subject into categories or parts, you must choose a principle of classification or division.

The principle may be simple (one criterion: e.g., classifying dogs by hair type) or complex (several criteria: classifying dogs by breed and uses). However, you must apply the principle consistently. You can write about herding dogs, retrievers, and lap dogs (uses), but not about herding dogs, long-haired dogs, and dogs from Wales (no consistent principle).

The following paragraph uses a complex principle to classify lies. The writer considers in each case why the liar lies and what others think of the liar.

Calling lies evil is not so simple, because there are really two types of lies. Most of us find the self-serving lie obnoxious. This lie serves to advance the liar's fortunes (sometimes at the expense of others), or to get him out of trouble. If we uncover the lie, we are likely to revile the liar. Others, however, lie to serve others and to make society run more smoothly, rather than to advance themselves. These "white lies" may make another person feel better, or protect an innocent party by covering up a misleading fact. At times we may even approve of this sort of lie.

What principle of division does the writer use in this paragraph about the liquid from which beer is made, called "wort"?

The ingredients used in making beer are boiled together in huge kettles; this mixture is called the wort. Each of the ingredients of the wort has a specific purpose. Malt, made from cooked barley grain, will give the finished beer body. Grains such as corn or wheat are changed in the wort from starch to sugar; as they ferment later on, they will provide the beer's alcoholic content. Brewers boil hops with the wort to give beer a slightly bitter flavor. Water, of course, provides volume.

E. Cause and Effect

The cause-and-effect paragraph generally develops from a cause to its effects, or from an effect to its causes. Sometimes, for reasons of emphasis, a writer will list a series of effects and end his paragraph with the cause (an inductive, or periodic, structure), or he may begin with a list of causes and end with a single effect. At times a cause-and-effect paragraph may shuttle back and forth: cause, effect; cause, effect. This sort of organization is appropriate when there is a chain-line connection between causes and effects, when an effect becomes a cause, and that cause has an effect that becomes another cause.

In most cases you will order your paragraph by proceeding from details of lesser importance to those of greater importance, or vice-versa (as in a newspaper article).

Here, in a paragraph by Dr. Benjamin Spock, causes and effects alternate:

After a baby is standing and walking, there's a real value in leaving him barefoot most of the time when conditions are suitable. A baby's arches are relatively flat at first. He gradually builds his arches up and strengthens his ankles by using them vigorously in standing and walking. (I suppose the reason that the soles of the feet are ticklish and sensitive under the arch is to remind us to keep that part arched up off the ground.) Walking on an uneven or rough surface also fosters the use of the foot and leg muscles. When you always provide a baby with a flat floor to walk on and always enclose his feet in shoes (with their smooth insides), especially if the soles are stiff, you encourage him to relax his foot muscles and to walk flat-footed.

A cause-and-effect structure lends itself to paragraphs in which a writer argues a case, or adopts a position. Notice that the topic sentence of the following paragraph occurs at the end; the paragraph is built from effects to cause.

Literacy and the desire to read are declining rapidly. The merchandising of gaudy materials is proceeding from the ugly to the subliminal; its effects on us are farther and farther from our control. Our ideologies are being shaped by glib, slickly-packaged news. More and more, passive receptivity is replacing initiative and healthful activity in our sports and entertainments. These are some of the effects that television is having on our society.

F. Comparison or Contrast

Structure and consistency are crucial in the development of a paragraph by comparison or contrast (or by both comparison and contrast). The two basic internal structures for such a paragraph are the block form and the shuttle form. Using the block form to compare A and B, you devote a section or paragraph to A; then you make a transition to B ("On the other hand, B . . ." or "Much like A, B . . .") and proceed to discuss in relation to B each of the points you raised about A. With the shuttle form, you pass back and forth from A to B, comparing them point-by-point as you go along. The block form is usually easier to write but harder to organize than the shuttle form; it often requires at least two paragraphs. The shuttle form lends itself more easily to complicated or detailed material.

Here Charles S. Brooks uses the shuttle method of contrast in an essay "On the Difference between Wit and Humor."

Wit is a lean creature with sharp inquiring nose, whereas humor has a kindly eye and comfortable girth. Wit, if it be necessary, uses malice to score a point — like a cat it is quick to jump — but humor keeps the peace in an easy chair. Wit has a better voice in a solo, but humor comes into the chorus best. Wit is as sharp as a stroke of lightning, whereas humor is diffuse like sunlight. Wit keeps the season's fashions and is precise in the phrases and judgements of the day, but humor is concerned with homely eternal things. Wit wears silk, but humor in homespun endures the wind. Wit sets a snare, whereas humor goes off whistling without a victim in its mind. Wit is sharper company at table, but humor serves better in mischance and in the rain. When it tumbles wit is sour, but humor goes uncomplaining without its dinner. Humor laughs at another's jest and holds its sides, while wit sits wrapped in study for a lively answer. But it is a workaday world in which we live, where we get mud upon our boots and come weary to the twilight — it is a world that grieves and suffers from many wounds in these years of war: and therefore as I think of my acquaintances it is those who are humorous in its best and truest meaning rather than those who are witty who give the more profitable companionship.

The following short paragraph on the preparation of fish uses the block method of paragraph development:

A careful chef will either steam or poach a delicate lean fish. Steaming is a simple process, although it results in some loss of weight. The steaming fish rests on a perforated tray above the boiling water. The lightly-greased poaching tray, on the other hand, is immersed in the simmering liquid (light stocks or bouillon may be used to add flavor). Poaching takes longer than steaming, but the fish loses little of its weight in the process.

G. Analogy

Analogy is a way to explain something unfamiliar to a reader by means of a comparison to something familiar. The comparison is not literal, though, as in a comparison-contrast paragraph. Here the things compared are essentially unlike, although they have similarities on which the analogy is based. These are similarities in relationships, not in appearances or qualities. For example, a helpful analogy devised by Fred Hoyle compared our expanding universe to a raisin cake baking in an oven. In size and appearance the universe and the cake could hardly be more different. Yet the relationships among their parts are strikingly similar: as both universe and cake expand from a center outward, the stars and raisins grow farther and farther apart. Comparison to a familiar (or at least easily comprehensible) process illustrates a phenomenon that would otherwise be hard for a non-physicist to grasp.

Of course, analogies have limits. In the previous example, the oven in which the cake bakes is small; space is infinite. Within its limits, though, the analogy is a powerful tool for illustration.

One caution: Because of the basic dissimilarity between its two sides an analogy is inappropriate in a logical argument.

In the following paragraph the writer uses a familiar animal to explain several characteristics of a political regime; he is using analogy.

> How does Gov. Harley's administration work? It works like a porcupine. Slow-moving and amiable, it lies low until some critic comes too close. Then it bristles with quills of innuendo and personal attacks, rolling up into a tight defensive ball. The Governor himself remains silent within his mansion, defended by a flow of barbed words from his aides. Most of the time he appears benevolent and interested in the state's welfare, but we must never forget that what he really wants is for us to leave him and his administration alone.

H. Analysis

Analysis is a general term for a paragraph in which the writer breaks his subject into parts. An analytical paragraph may use classification, cause and effect, comparison, or other methods of development.

Grant Arnold creates an analysis paragraph to distinguish among three types of presses in *Creative Lithography*.

> In graphic art printing three types of presses are in use. Each press is designed for its own particular kind of printing. The press used for printing wood engravings exerts a downward pressure and presses the printing paper against the raised portions of the inked, engraved block to make the impression. The etching press is operated by causing the copper plate to travel on a bed between steel rollers that exert a rolling two-way pressure which forces the printing paper into the lines of the etching. The print is made by the paper pulling the ink from the incised lines on the plate. The lithograph press uses a

still different kind of pressure. The pressure is obtained by a lever that forces the stone on the press bed against the scraper fixed in the scraper box suspended in the frame of the press. When the bed is moved by means of a crank handle, it is carried over a heavy steel roller. The scraper, resting on a greased tympan covering the stone, forces the printing paper against the printing ink. The ink is scraped from the stone to the paper to make the print.

Exercises

A. 1. Examine the list of topics in No. 2 below. Indicate for each one which method of paragraph development would be most appropriate.

2. Write opening paragraphs for any three of the topics below. Each paragraph should clearly indicate which method of development you are following. You may invent details.

   a. Trace the influence of the Beatles on popular music.

   b. Discuss the various masks people wear to hide their feelings from others.

   c. Agree or disagree: The Republican Party is closer to the mainstream of contemporary American social thought than is the Democratic Party.

   d. Explain the structure of minor league baseball.

   e. How do television signals travel from the transmitting antenna?

   f. What is a blunderbuss?

   g. Tanzania's problems are typical of those faced by African states struggling for economic stability. Discuss.

B. Here is Ernest Boyd's informal definition of the "Aesthete: Model 1924." In a paragraph of your own, informally define a "type" which is prevalent today.

He is a child of this Twentieth Century, for the Yellow Nineties had flickered out in the delirium of the Spanish-American War when his first gurgles rejoiced the ears of his expectant parents. If Musset were more than a name to him, a hazy recollection of French literature courses, he might adapt a line from the author of *La Confession d'un Enfant du Siecle* and declare: I came too soon into a world too old. But no such doubts trouble his spirit, for he believes that this century is his because he was born with it. He does not care who makes its laws, so long as he makes its literature. To this important task he has consecrated at least three whole years of his conscious — or rather self-conscious — existence, and nothing, as yet, has happened to shake his faith in his star. In fact, he finds the business rather easier than he anticipated when, in the twilight sleep of the classroom, vague reports reached him of Milton's infinitesimal fee for

"Paradise Lost," of Chatterton's death, of the harassed lives of Shelley and Keats, of the eternal struggle of the artist against the indifference of his age and the foul bludgeonings of fate.

C. What is the principle of classification in this paragraph by Robert Hertzberg? Is it simple or complex?

Messages having secret or hidden meaning are called *cryptograms*. There are two distinct varieties. In the *code type* (the word "code" having nothing whatsoever to do with the dits and dahs of International Morse), altogether different meanings are assigned to intelligible complete words, phrases, and sentences. This must be done by pre-arrangement between the sender of the message and the recipient. A message might read, "Oceans of love and best wishes for a pleasant crossing," and by itself it makes sense and appears to be innocent. However, the person receiving it might understand it to mean, "Dump the diamonds overboard. Someone has squealed to Customs." For less sinister commercial purposes there exist fat books of *code lists* whose purpose is economy rather than deception. For instance, the single word "boy" might mean "Arriving in Baltimore," or "girl" might mean "Your order received." When you pay 25 or 50 cents a word for overseas transmission, you want to use as few as possible!

In a paragraph of your own, classify "fools" or "advertisements." Make sure your principle is clear before you begin.

D. Here are some topics for paragraphs to develop by one or more of the methods you have studied:

1. Describe a food, tool, or household item without naming it. By the end of your paragraph the reader should be able to identify the object from your description of its shape, texture, feel, taste, and use.

2. Paint a word-picture of one wall of a building. Be sure your description proceeds smoothly from one detail to another.

3. Explain how to make a simple paper airplane from an 8½ by 11 inch sheet of paper. Assume that your reader has never seen such an airplane. Be sure the directions you give are clear and logical.

4. Complete a paragraph which begins: "The smell of a new car (or a new book, or new shoes) is like . . . ." Carry your analogy through the whole paragraph.

5. Divide teachers into three major "types." Make sure your principle of division is consistent through the paragraph.

6. Develop: A rich, spoiled childhood affects the future adult. In this paragraph coherent development is especially challenging.

7. Define a current slang term which students apply to either the idol or the outcast in school.

8. Describe the way your English classroom empties when the class is over. Be sure to find a consistent plan of organization.

9. Complete a paragraph which begins: "On a November afternoon I witnessed the *death of the year.*" Extend the metaphor through the whole paragraph.

10. Define the noun *geziddelunk*. The word has no dictionary definition.

III.
The Composition

Writing as Proof

Limiting and Developing a Topic

The Outline

Some Structural Patterns for the Composition

Opening Lines

Closing Lines

I. Papa, Squam Lake - II, 1973   Kelly Wise

Writing as Proof

A good writer understands the several steps in written communication: he or she must

1. *state* a clear thesis,
2. *develop* the thesis,
3. *convince* the reader.

Successful completion of the first two steps establishes the reader's understanding of and confidence in the writer — a necessity for convincing communication. Writing is thus a process of working out a *proof*. The writer proves his case by stating his core contention (or argument) first, and then supporting it with relevant and sufficient evidence. So structured, good writing informs and convinces the reader.

On the other hand, if the thesis is cloudy, or the development is sketchy, then the proof is unconvincing; good communication has not taken place.

The process of working out a proof is simply stated, but it is not easily mastered. The ability to state a thesis clearly, and to phrase that thesis so that it indicates the direction that the writer intends to follow, is not easy to attain; nor is the knack of sound, complete, convincing development.

These skills depend on good thinking. The shape of the proof must be clear in the writer's mind, or it will not be clear to the reader. Of course, a writer may do well to "think" on paper by listing ideas, making outlines, or experimenting with rough drafts; but before he begins to write the actual composition, his thought process must produce both a clear sense of the central thesis and a specific direction for development.

Although good thinking is a requisite of good writing, it is not the only requisite. Good thinking provides an organization for the composition, but it does not assure communication between writer and reader. Even a well-structured proof is unconvincing unless it is framed in an original, lively piece of writing. Therefore, when a writer moves from a paragraph to a longer composition, he should attend not only to the need for sound, organized thinking but also to the skills and techniques that help him achieve convincing communication through development of a vigorous personal prose style.

Limiting and Developing a Topic

Choosing a Topic

Careful choice of your topic, the central subject of the composition, is vital. You must define it clearly in your own mind; it must not be so broad as to make thorough development of it impossible, nor so narrow as to preclude any development at all. Once you have limited the topic, you must develop it fully.

Here the general topic "War" is limited, step by step.

1. War
2. Weapons of war
3. Medieval weapons
4. Large medieval weapons
5. The catapult
6. Uses of the catapult

Whereas "weapons of war" could be properly developed only by a whole book, "the catapult" might be developed by a short composition, and "uses of the catapult" by a single paragraph.

Thesis Statement

Once you have chosen and carefully planned (and perhaps outlined) your topic, you should create a thesis statement. The thesis statement must be an accurate assertion of the content of the composition. It must not be too broad in scope (including ideas the work should not deal with), or too narrow in focus (omitting some of the important ideas in the work). It must be strictly relevant. A strong thesis statement is a great aid to your reader, and it helps you organize your ideas as you begin to write the composition.

Developing a Topic

Proper development of a topic means treating in full all of the ideas implied by the thesis statement and treating only those ideas. If, for example, you are writing a critical paper whose topic sentence is "Shakespeare's *Hamlet*, contrary to current belief, is a comedy more than a tragedy," you must be careful to develop both parts of the assertion. If the composition points out the com-

J. Untitled   **Eugene Richards**

edy in the play without discussing the tragedy, development is narrow and incomplete. If the essay considers another play as well as *Hamlet*, development is too broad. If the essay deals extensively with details from Shakespeare's life, its development is digressive. Proper development of the topic indicated by the thesis statement would include discussion of the play both as a tragedy and as a comedy, and perhaps discussion of "current belief."

The Outline

The outline provides a means of organizing your ideas before you actually begin to write. The best way to begin is to jot down a list of ideas that pertain to your topic. Here is a short list of ideas that might be useful in developing the topic "Wastefulness in America":

Wastefulness
   multiple wrappers
   rubber tires in dumps
   "gas guzzlers"
   plastic "bubbles" on merchandise
   no recycling
   one-person-one-car commuters

If time is short (for instance, if you are taking a timed test), this may be the only form of outline that you have time to make. Your next step would be to construct a thesis statement; then you would develop that statement with the ideas on the list.

If you have enough time, however, it is helpful to organize the ideas in the rough list. Here is one scheme of organization for the short list on wastefulness:

Wastefulness
   rubber tires in dumps
   "gas guzzlers"
   one-person-one-car commuters

   multiple wrappers
   plastic "bubbles" on merchandise

   inadequate recycling

   wind & water & sun power

Now the composition has a shape. The writer will begin with a vivid image (the tires in dumps) and reinforce that image with other examples of wastefulness associated with the automobile. Another paragraph will discuss wasteful packaging; then the writer will move to possible solutions: recycling, and alternative forms of power.

The longer and more complex your topic is, the more likely it is that a more formal outline will help you organize your ideas. Here are two traditional kinds of outlines, the topic outline and the paragraph outline, used to organize ideas for a facetious argument:

Topic Outline

Thesis: Grass should be plowed under, and all of our lawns should be
be covered with Astroturf or macadam.

I. Problem of lawn grass
   A. Maintenance
      1. water shortages
      2. rising fuel costs
   B. Control of weed growth
      1. fuel cost
      2. harmful weed-killers

II. Health hazards
   A. Mosquitoes and other insects
      1. breeding places
      2. pesticide dangers
   B. Allergies
   C. Injuries
      1. heart attacks
      2. severed toes
   D. Two-cycle engine pollution

III. Benefits of alternative lawn coverings
   A. Clean air
   B. Multiple uses
      1. parking
      2. game courts
         a. basketball
         b. volleyball
   C. Uniform color
   D. No mowing (conclusion)

Notice the thesis statement at the beginning of the outline. It must begin the paragraph outline, too. In addition, the paragraph outline includes a topic sentence for each paragraph. From the paragraph outline it is a very short step to the finished draft.

Paragraph Outline

Thesis statement: Grass should be plowed under and all of our lawns covered with Astroturf or macadam.

Topic Sentence 1: America is faced with a worsening problem in the maintenance and control of lawn grass.

    Water shortage

    Growth of unattractive weeds

    Unproductive use of leisure time

Topic Sentence 2: Lawns and their care create serious health hazards for Americans.

    Breeding mosquitoes
    Allergies

    Heart attacks and severed toes

    Two-cycle engine pollution

Topic Sentence 3: Coverings other than grass provide more sanitary, useful, attractive and economical surfaces for our outdoor areas.

    Clean air
    Parking
    Basketball courts
    Uniform green color
    No mowing

Exercise

Organize the following details into an outline:

Machu Picchu

called the lost city of the Incas

discovered in 1911 by a Yale professor, Hiram Bingham

75 miles north of Cuzco, Peru

Bingham declared it was the lost city that scholars had spoken of

he published an article, "The Lost City of the Incas"

after the Spanish laid siege to Cuzco in the early 16th century, the Incas fled

3000 feet above the Urubamba River

Incas built their homes there

highest spot, Temple of the Sun

temples and farming terraces

they were sun worshipers

Temple of the Chosen Women

100 or more perfectly hewn stone stairways

absolutely invisible to anyone below

a marvel how the large stones, some weighing more than a ton, were brought up there

set upon a plateau on a mountain

hidden in a lush valley of the Andes

often cloaked in wisps of clouds

the Peruvian government was embarrassed by Bingham's discovery

terraces designed, each about 4 feet apart, to retain rainwater

Bingham found many skeletons there, mostly women

one theory is that Machu Picchu was a sanctuary for Inca women and children

Exercises

A. Create from each of the following general ideas topics narrow enough for appropriate development in a composition of 3 - 5 paragraphs, and then in a single paragraph.

1.	clothes	6.	English
2.	the double standard	7.	politics
3.	football	8.	music
4.	Canada	9.	highways
5.	courage	10.	the telephone

Next choose any one of the topics, and make notes on what you would include in the 3 - 5 paragraph composition, and in the single paragraph.

B. Below is a list of details concerning "The Affair of the Diamond Necklace," a scandal in the French court which took place several years before the French Revolution. What might be an interesting way to begin if you were to write an account of the affair? Which of these details would you select for topic sentences? What methods of paragraph development would you expect to use? Make a topic outline from the details.

1. scandal occurred 1784-1786
2. Marie Antoinette was Queen
3. the Cardinal de Rohan was persuaded to buy a diamond necklace for the Queen to earn her favor
4. the Queen disliked Rohan because of his anti-Austrian views
5. A Mme. Lamotte, posing as a countess, convinced Rohan to buy the necklace
6. Rohan bought the necklace on the installment plan in the Queen's name
7. Rohan couldn't keep up payments, and the jewelers prosecuted
8. Mme. Lamotte's husband absconded to England with the necklace
9. M. Lamotte made a fortune by breaking up the necklace and selling the diamonds
10. at the trial in 1785 Rohan was acquitted
11. Mme. Lamotte was imprisoned, but later escaped
12. the Queen had no part in the scandal, but it was linked to her
13. the scandal appeared indicative of the moral decay of the court of Marie Antoinette
14. everybody involved got what was coming to him or her

Some Structural Patterns for the Composition

There is probably an infinite number of ways to develop an essay. Here are only a few.

1. Question — Answer
Francis Bacon began a celebrated essay with a question: "What is truth? said jesting Pilate; and would not stay for an answer." In adopting this essay pattern, Bacon took two long paragraphs to offer his view of truth. When you use this pattern, beware of littering your essay with other questions.

2. Quotation — Explication
A significant quotation or excerpts from a passage appear in the introduction. After signifying the difficult sections of the passage, perhaps mentioning some of the standard interpretations of them, you proceed with your interpretation.

3. The Frame
The beginning and ending of the composition frame the body. A vignette, analogy, or pertinent quotation may be used. In the final paragraph the writer takes us back, reminds us of the beginning, without obvious repetition. Such a technique enables him to make, perhaps, one further point, or at the very least to end on a familiar theme or on an established rhythm or tone.

4. Classification — Division
As in a lawyer's brief, facts are central to this pattern: no gloss, very little style or literary flair. Classification or division sets the order. The thesis statement establishes the subject to be defended or substantiated. The paragraphs follow from this statement logically: one, two, three, four. Often the last paragraph reaffirms the thesis statement. Neither in this pattern nor in the frame is the conclusion a mere repetition of the opening paragraph or the thesis sentence.

5. Past/Present: What Is/What Can or Should Be
The introduction and succeeding paragraphs establish a background for the subject of the essay. The body of the essay concerns

the present or what according to the writer can or should occur. This pattern can be employed with the frame.

6. Objections/Overriding Advantages

This structure opens with a discussion of the obvious objections to whatever the writer is proposing. The rest of the composition supports the thesis by showing all of the advantages of the proposal, advantages which override the obvious objections.

Opening Lines

Often the opening lines of an essay establish a pattern to be developed. Do you recognize any pattern that might be suggested by these openings?

1. When Charlie Parker died in New York on March 12, 1955, he left us a tradition and sound that may live forever. The names of cities and artists that cluster about his personal history have indeed become some of the signposts that chart the history of Jazz.

2. Criticism is a study by which men grow important and formidable at a very small expense. (Samuel Johnson, "The Idler," No. 60)

3. It is said that the world is in a state of bankruptcy, that the world owed the world more than the world can pay, and ought to go into chancery, and be sold. (Ralph Waldo Emerson, "Gifts")

4. After years of spoofing psychiatrists as charlatans and clever businessmen, I find myself in the embarrassing position of praising at least one "shrink." I continue to believe that there is considerable evidence to support my earlier attitude toward psychiatry: however, in the case of Robert and Dr. Bligh (pseudonyms, of course) I must retract many of my harshest criticisms.

5. There is a gross misunderstanding about women's clothing. Fashion designers, runs the argument, abuse us with their creations. Although we may prefer our skirts long, if they decree that short skirts are the fashion of the day, what can we say? Poppycock! That's what I say.

6. Men are ruled by imagination: imagination makes them into men, capable of madness and of immense labours. (George Santayana, "Imagination")

7. There is a kind of charity that oppresses our society.

There are at least two types of openings that you should avoid:

1. The Digressive Opening: A student writing, for example, on the symbolism of architecture in Henry James's *The Portrait of a Lady* may be tempted to begin his essay with a summary of Henry James's life or literary career, or with an attempted survey of American literature or of European architecture. Such an opening is digressive and irrelevant, and suggests both poor organization and the writer's fear of the topic. Simply begin with a direct, relevant statement that may even be your

K. Untitled, 1972   **Steve Wicks**

thesis statement: "Architecture plays a symbolic role in Henry James's novel *The Portrait of a Lady* . . ."

2. The Dictionary Opening: "Webster (or "The dictionary") defines *symbolism* as . . ." is a trite, formulaic opening that every English teacher confronts at least a dozen times a year. Vary your openings; work your definitions into your essay in a more subtle, original way.

Closing Lines

Many students are convinced that they must end each essay with a crashing climax like the end of a Beethoven symphony. Such an instinct is noble but unrealistic. Although a brilliant ending may occasionally occur to you, it is far more reasonable to strive simply for a strong, logical conclusion. Knowing your conclusion before you begin writing will also increase your confidence, and will therefore almost infallibly improve your writing style.

But do not tolerate a weak ending. "I hope I have proved that the North and the South had distinctly different economic problems in the years preceding the Civil War," is far too weak. If the writer is not convinced that he has clearly proved a point, what chance is there for the reader to be convinced? Rephrase the sentence, omitting the entire sentiment about "hoping"; and if the sentence merely repeats an earlier statement, omit this final sentence altogether.

A powerful instinct to overcome is the urge to find a formula for endings. Formulas produce dullness and repetition. The worst manifestation of the formula is something like "In conclusion, let me repeat (or summarize) . . . ." A duller ending would be hard to imagine. If you have stated your point articulately the first time, there is no need to repeat it; if you have stated your point obscurely or clumsily the first time, go back and rewrite it.

Yet another weakness is the leap into a *non sequitur* in the closing sentence or paragraph. "Thus, Polonius's consciously malevolent actions together with the effects of his death make *Hamlet* a multi-leveled and exciting play." The writer of that sentence probably discussed thoroughly the many ways in which Polonius affects the play *Hamlet* both before and after his death; but if she has not proved that Polonius makes the play "multi-leveled and exciting," she has created a closing sentence that sounds rather impressive but is actually a *non sequitur*. She is implying that her essay achieves more than it in fact does.

Instead of formulas, consider some guidelines when you are having difficulty writing your ending:

1. Maybe pure logic will suggest the conclusion. As you argue your way from point *a* to point *f*, point *f* is your natural con-

clusion. Simply end with that natural climax (e.g., "I find it impossible, therefore, to support Mr. Smith's candidacy.")

2. One difficult but admirable goal when you are writing under pressure, as you would on an examination essay, is to end with your most important idea: the outgrowth of your reasoning, but neither repetition nor a new idea-out-of-nowhere.

3. Perhaps your essay now leads to broader considerations. Suggest them. ("If the Supreme Court rules in favor of Sanderson, we leave it to our readers to infer what will happen to the privacy of the mails.")

4. Occasionally a quotation will make your point more dramatically and succinctly than your own words can (see the passage below by Maynard Mack).

5. Sometimes a rhetorical device works well. Consider the inversion that ends the following paragraph from *The New Yorker* of 20 June 1977:

> The jazz saxophonist Paul Desmond, who died a week or so ago, at the age of fifty-two, once remarked that the sound he tried to achieve on the alto saxophone might be compared to a dry Martini. The quote followed him for years, and he would sometimes gently point out to whoever brought it up that he'd gone on to say that his playing often sounded like several dry Martinis. But, of course, it did not. His clean, flutelike tone was always perfectly controlled — bittersweet, slightly wistful, and very much the mirror of a romantic inner self he kept mostly hidden, in day-to-day life, behind a lightning wit. Desmond was fascinated by counterpoint in jazz — the spontaneous flow of interweaving lines conjured up right on the stand, from moment to moment — and part of his admiration for Dave Brubeck, his partner for seventeen years, was based on that fascination. Brubeck and Desmond were able to do counterpoint almost immediately, the second time they played together, and Desmond considered this both a miracle and a mystery. For many years, Desmond lived alone in a small apartment in midtown Manhattan, surrounded by a seemingly unchanging clutter of books, records, tape recorders, earphones, and sheet music. He had lots of money, but it didn't appear to interest him. He liked good bars, puzzles of all kinds, puns, and staying up all night. The things he disliked he kept to himself.

Here are some closing sentences from distinguished writers.

And though Hemingway has not given — and never intended to give — a documented diagnosis of our age, he has given us one of the most compelling symbols of a personal response to our age. (Robert Penn Warren, "Ernest Hemingway")

A Baltimorean is not merely John Doe, an isolated individual of *Homo sapiens*, exactly like every other John Doe. He is John Doe *of* a certain place — of Baltimore, of a definite *house* in Baltimore. It is not by accident that all the people of Europe, very early in their history, distinguished their best men by adding *of* this or that place to their names. (H.L. Mencken, "On Living in Baltimore")

He [Hamlet] accepts the world as it is, the world as a duel, in which whether we know it or not, evil holds the poisoned rapier and the poisoned chalice waits; and in which, if we win at all, it costs not less than everything. I think we understand by the close of Shakespeare's *Hamlet* why it is that unlike the other tragic heroes he is given a soldier's rites upon the stage. For as William Butler Yeats once said, "Why should we honor those who die on the field of battle? A man may show as reckless a courage in entering into the abyss of himself." (Maynard Mack, "The World of *Hamlet*")

Man must, and will, use his environment. He should not use it up. An ecological budget which is unbalanced for too long endangers the physical and spiritual well-being, in fact the very existence of our future generations. It also endangers the future of the many other living things which share the planet with us and which have taught us so much about ourselves and about the nature of life itself. (John W. Kimball, *Biology*)

Topics for Compositions

1. In America, we greet each other by shaking hands; in Peru, the gesture is different: an embrace, followed by a gentle thumping on the back. Each society has its "tribal rites." Choose a modern rite you recognize in our society or in another; explain the enactment and effects of that rite. You may wish to contrast the rite you have chosen with another one from modern or ancient society.

2. Adopt a space somewhere in your environment — a street corner, the entrance to a library, the rear section of a bus — and record your impressions of that place. You may write in either the first or third person. Seek details that will allow the reader to know this space through your sense impressions; arrange the details in a coherent order, according to a scheme.

3. Alexis de Tocqueville, a Frenchman visiting America, wrote in 1835: "America is the land of wonders, in which everything is in constant motion and every change seems an improvement." Apply de Tocqueville's statement to the America of the 1970s. How would society today look to a visitor? Would the enthusiasm in the author's statement be justified today? Why or why not?

4. Clichés are statements or phrases that were once descriptive and have become stale and unemphatic by overuse. Yet closely scrutinized, or turned inside-out by a clever writer, clichés may disclose surprising truths or unexpected humor. Choose a cliché — "He laughs best who laughs last," "The early bird gets the worm," "Step on a crack, break your mother's back," or another — and write a wry, whimsical composition of several paragraphs which views the cliché in a novel way.

5. A news story reports only certain details of an event, and organizes these details in order of importance. Life is not so neatly arranged as the news. Invent a narrative or descriptive action for a news item you have recently read. Limit yourself to a very little dialogue; concentrate on description and characterization. Use active, lively verbs. Draft this action in the first person. (You might also write it later in the third person, to observe the differences between first and third person.)

6. Select a political cartoon from a magazine or newspaper. List in an outline the ways in which the portrayal of the cartoon differs from a real-life situation or photograph of the person or scene depicted. Then in a composition explain how a political cartoonist makes his effect, using the cartoon and your list for examples.

7. Think of a song that you particularly like or dislike and that has some sort of effect on you. In a composition organized by a strong thesis statement, explain the effect on you of the music and of the lyrics.

8. Write down a recent remark or statement which really irritated you. The source might be a friend, a television broadcast, a newspaper story. Using that remark or statement as a starting point, in a composition of several paragraphs explain (if the statement itself does not make it clear) the statement's meaning; then either attack the statement or explain why you believe the speaker made it.

9. Write a three-paragraph characterization of a person about whom you have mixed emotions (see, for example, the single paragraph about Miss Gowrie by Mary McCarthy, Supplemental Material #10). Remember that the trivial detail that sticks in your mind is just the sort of device that will probably capture your reader's interest as well.

10. Write an editorial about a crisis (community, national, or international) that should have affected our lives, conduct, and outlook — but failed to do so. Some examples from the 1970s are a political scandal or upheaval, a civil war overseas, and an international crisis.

11. Choose a magazine or periodical which appeals to a certain distinct group (examples are *Yachting*, *Popular Electronics*, *People*, *Spiderman* comics). For an audience that would be unfamiliar with this magazine, define and characterize the magazine in an essay of several paragraphs. Avoid the jargon of the magazine's special field.

12. Today newspapers face many problems: competition from other media (radio and television), rising expenses, the daily pressure of time, labor disputes. Have daily newspapers outlived their usefulness? Are they doomed, or will they survive? Explain your views in several clearly-organized paragraphs.

13. After reading Katherine Anne Porter's paragraph about Frau Hutten on page 93, write a characterization in which you praise someone for the wrong reasons, thus intentionally satirizing your subject.

14. Condense a long article in a magazine or newspaper to three or four paragraphs. Omit none of the important ideas in the original passage; beware of inserting new ideas; use appropriate diction.

IV.
The Writer's Voice

First Person, Third Person, Persona

Audience and Voice

Kinds of Diction

Denotation and Connotation

Figurative Language

Style

M. Untitled   Eugene Richards

First Person, Third Person, Persona

First person, using the identifiable *I* as speaker or narrator, has freshness and immediacy. We think we know who is speaking; we feel perhaps that we too are there describing the event, making the evaluation. Subjectivity is built into this form of writing. Were any one of us recording the same event, our perceptions might be quite different. There is, however, an obvious danger in using the first person. Some authority and objectivity are sacrificed, whereas using the third person supposes that the speaker or narrator is an authority, whose word need not be questioned.

Recollections, personal essays, events that you witness or participate in: these are ordinarily written in the first person. Reports, analyses, arguments: these are often written in the third person. Narratives can be written in either person.

Here is an example of the use of first person by John Barth in *The Floating Opera*. Note the immediacy and subjectivity of the paragraph.

> May I say that I am perhaps the best lawyer on the Eastern Shore? Perhaps I shouldn't, for you'll take the statement as self-praise. If I thought the practice of law absolutely important, then my statement would indeed be as much a boast as a description; but truthfully I consider advocacy, jurisprudence, even justice, to have no more intrinsic importance than, say, oyster-shucking. And you'd understand, wouldn't you, that if a man like myself asserted with a smile that he was the peninsula's best oyster shucker (I'm not), or cigarette roller, or pinball-machine tilter, he'd not be guilty of prideful boasting? It requires small subtlety to grasp that, I think.

The following paragraph from *Go Tell It on the Mountain*, by James Baldwin, employs the third person. It could have been rendered in the first person. What reasons led the writer to cast it instead in the third person?

> And after death's first silent vigil her life came to her bedside to curse her with many voices. Her mother, in rotting rags and filling the room with the stink of the grave, stood over her to curse the daughter who had denied her on her deathbed. Gabriel came, from all his times and ages, to curse the sister who had held him to scorn and mocked her in her pain and barrenness. Frank came, even he, with that same smile, the same tilt of his head. Of them all she would have begged forgiveness, had they come with ears to hear.

But they came like many trumpets; even if they had come to hear and not to testify it was not they who could forgive her, but only God.

For certain reasons a writer may wish to choose a mask, or *persona*. A satirist may use a persona to applaud the very position he deplores, counting on the reader to detect the folly of that position. On the other hand, the character created by the writer may exhibit certain contrived liabilities as a narrator — because he is so innocent, like the narrator in Twain's *Huckleberry Finn*; or because he is so disaffected, like Holden Caulfield in *The Catcher in the Rye* — that the writer puts to strong advantage.

Particularly in the study of literature you should be aware of the subtleties that the writer can achieve through persona (i.e., the character posed as narrator). A first person narrator may imply that he is telling you the truth and nothing but the truth. He may seem unspeakably honest. Yet you must be suspicious; you must wait. For you know that objectivity in this world is rare indeed. In the hands of a skillful writer, a persona may reveal much about himself and his narrative by obvious omissions or contradictions or discrepencies between what he reports and what later we understand truly has happened.

Consider the obvious difference between the poet and the persona in the following poem:

Epigram. Engraved on the Collar of a Dog which I gave to his Royal Highness.

> I am his Highness' Dog at *Kew;*
> Pray tell me Sir, whose Dog are you?
> — Alexander Pope

The opening paragraph of *Moby Dick* is a famous example of the use of persona.

Call me Ishmael. Some years ago — never mind how long precisely — having little or no money in my purse and nothing particular to interest me on shore, I thought I would sail about a little and see the watery part of the world. It is a way I have of driving off the spleen and regulating the circulation. Whenever I find myself growing grim about the mouth; whenever it is a damp, drizzly November in my soul; whenever I find myself involuntarily pausing before coffin warehouses, and bringing up the rear of every funeral I meet; and especially whenever my hypos* get such an upper hand of me, that it requires a strong moral principle to prevent me from deliberately stepping into the street, and methodically knocking people's hats off — then, I account it high time to get to sea as soon as I can. This is my substitute for pistol and ball. With a philosophical flourish Cato throws himself upon his sword; I quietly take to the ship. There is nothing surprising in this. If they but knew it, almost all men in their degree, some time or other, cherish very nearly the same feelings toward the ocean with me.

How would you describe the narrative voice in this paragraph? What characteristic of personality is Herman Melville giving to Ishmael, his persona? How do "sail about a little and see the watery part of the world" and "with a philosophical flourish Cato throws himself upon his sword" contribute to the reader's impression of Ishmael?

*hypos: hypochondria, melancholy

Audience and Voice

No writer works in a vacuum; what he produces is meant to be read. If it is to be understood, it must be written with the readers for whom it is intended in mind. Indeed, there is a subtle contract between writer and reader in everything that is written. By his words and structure, the writer announces to his readers (his audience) the authority from which he writes, his attitude toward his readers, and his attitude toward his subject. He may also show us that he chooses to wear a mask, to employ the persona.

If you are instructing a seven-year-old to assemble a balsa plane from a cereal package, you will want to use simple words, elementary syntax, and several drawings. If, on the other hand, you are writing a literary explication for a college seminar, you will want to use words and structures that are capable of conveying subtlety of meaning to an intellectual mind. If you are writing a letter to your maiden aunt, you will probably use different words and more formal structure than you would use if writing to someone your own age. Suiting your writing style to your audience helps you write efficiently. Be sure, therefore, to identify your audience before you begin to write.

The speaker's voice that a writer adopts is determined partly by his conception of the reader and partly by the knowledge and authority that the writer creates for the voice. The writer may be an expert in nuclear physics writing to an audience of high school students. Naturally, if he wishes to communicate he should assume that his readers are unfamiliar with the sophisticated vocabulary of the physicist. Thus, he will be inclined to seek a diction level that they can readily understand and to phrase simple definitions of the theories and axioms of his field. Or the writer may speak in a voice that lacks the assurance of the specialist. He might speak as a common citizen to fellow citizens about an issue to be discussed in Town Meeting. His ideas may be considered as opinion and fact addressed to an audience that shares common knowledge of the subject. Emotion can be conveyed through the writer's voice: anger, outrage, compassion, concern.

The intended audience dictates the voice in the following advertisement. What are the audience and voice in this passage?

You can first-night at a performance of Tosca in one of the world's most acoustically perfect theaters. Or groove to a rock concert in the sweet air. There's a great cultural center where you can explore Polynesia's multi-colored past. And a magnificent aquatic museum where her future is on display.

In Hawaii you'll find out what it's like to speak in a different language, worship in a different church, even live in a different colored skin.

So before you go anywhere in this world, talk to your travel agent. He'll tell you it's all happening in Hawaii.

Kinds of Diction

Choose the appropriate kind of diction for your writing. Appropriateness depends on the subject matter, the situation, and the audience for which you are writing. The language of Shakespeare, for instance, would not be used for a seventh-grade geography lesson; nor would the vocabulary of "Dick and Jane" be sufficient to explain concepts in nuclear physics. Once you have found the appropriate kind of diction, be consistent in your use of it. Do not change from one kind of diction to another, unless you mean to prove a point by doing so.

There are many kinds of diction, each appropriate to a certain subject, context, and audience. Below are examples of only four kinds. Examine the authors' choices of words to determine the differences between them.

1. Relatively formal diction characterizes this paragraph from George Steiner's *The Death of Tragedy*.

   There is in every literary movement a part of revolt and a part of tradition. Romanticism arose in rebellion against the ideals of reason and rational form which had governed taste in the late seventeenth and eighteenth centuries. In the mythology of Blake the wings of imagination are liberated from the cold blight of reason put upon them by Newton and Voltaire. The poetics of romanticism were necessarily polemic, being elaborated in the course of an attack on neo-classic principles. Wordsworth's Preface to the *Lyrical Ballads* and Victor Hugo's critical manifestoes are at once proclamations of future intent and explicit condemnations of the immediate literary past. Had Pope and Voltaire not existed the romantics would have had to invent them in order to articulate their own contrary values.

2. This paragraph, written by John Updike in *The New Yorker*, uses a chatty, informal kind of diction:

   We recently had a carpenter build a few things in our house in the country. It's an old house, leaning away from the wind a little; its floors sag gently, like an old mattress. The carpenter turned his back on our tilting walls and took his vertical from a plumb line and his horizontal from a bubble level, and then went to work by the light of these absolutes. Fitting his planks into place took a lot of those long, irregular, oblique cuts with a ripsaw that break an amateur's heart. The bookcase and kitchen counter and cabinet he left behind stand perfectly up-and-down in a cockeyed house. Their rectitude is chastening. For minutes at a stretch, we study them, wondering if perhaps it isn't, after all, the wall that is true and the bookcase that leans. Eventually, we suppose, everything will settle into the comfortably crooked, but it will take years, barring earthquakes, and in the meantime we are annoyed at being made to live with impossible standards.

3. In a selection from *The Kandy-Kolored Tangerine-Flake Streamline Baby* Tom Wolfe uses a jazzy, colloquial list of words to create a scene:

   Banges manes bouffants beehives Beatle caps butter faces brush-on lashes decal eyes puffy sweaters French thrust bras flailing leather blue jeans stretch jeans honeydew bottoms eclair shanks elf boots ballerinas Knight slippers, hundred of them, these flaming little buds, bobbing and screaming, rocketing around inside the Academy of Music Theater underneath that vast old mouldering cherub dome up there — aren't they super-marvelous!

   "Aren't they super-marvelous!" says Baby Jane, and then: "Hi, Isabel! Isabel! You want to sit backstage — with the Stones!"

   The show hasn't even started yet, the Rolling Stones aren't even on the stage, the place is full of a great shabby mouldering dimness, and these flaming little buds.

4. Jargon denotes a special diction belonging to a certain group: the government, the military, scientists, literary critics, and street gangs all use specialized vocabularies. Jargon does not communicate ideas efficiently to a general audience. How much of this paragraph from *The Radio Amateur's Handbook* is intelligible to the average reader?

   Couplers of this type are beneficial in the reduction of harmonic energy from the transmitter, an aid to TVI reduction. It should be possible to realize a 30-dB-or-greater decrease in harmonic level by using this Transmatch between the transmitter and the feed line. When connected ahead of a receiver as well — a common arrangement — the added selectivity of the coupler's tuned circuits will help to reduce images and other undesired receiver responses from out-of-band signals. The built-in Monimatch-type SWR indicator enables the operator to tune the Transmatch for minimum reflected power, assuring a good match between the transmitter and the feed line. . . .

Denotation and Connotation

Denotation is the pure, simple dictionary definition of a word, devoid of any personal or emotional associations. It is difficult to find a completely denotative word (except for conjunctions and prepositions) because of mental and emotional associations that are either universal or personal. A scientific symbol (H_2O) stands a better chance of being wholly denotative than a word does.

Connotation is the shade of meaning that has accrued to a word through use. Connotation is a valuable fact of language: it enlarges our vocabulary, provides fine and accurate distinctions, and helps the writer to appeal to the emotions as well as to the intellect.

Here are some examples of connotation:

Slim and *slender* are connotatively complimentary.

Thin is almost neutral, probably complimentary in America.

Skinny is derogatory — and connotative.

Yet any of these adjectives could be applied to the same person, depending on the speaker's attitude toward the person.

The connotations of some words are governed by context:

Richard is taking a course in *adolescent* psychology. (neutral: denotative)

Richard's *adolescent* reaction to the joke embarrassed everyone. (pejorative: connotative)

A more extreme example of the same pattern:

Mother bought a delicious leg of lamb from the *butcher*.

Although the content of Ellen's term paper was acceptable, she *butchered* the English language.

What is the narrator's joke on himself in this passage from Henry Fielding's *Joseph Andrews?*

. . . it becomes an author generally to divide a book as it does a butcher to joint his meat, for such assistance is of great help to both reader and the carver.

The connotations of other words may depend on idiom and metaphor. The simple word *blue*, for instance, has many different connotations; in some cases frequent use of the connotation has almost converted that meaning into denotation. *Blue* can connote

a) pornography (blue movie)
b) female intellectualism (bluestocking)
c) aristocracy (blue blood)
d) puritan (bluenose, blue laws)
e) melancholy (blue mood)
f) melancholy jazz (from the above, in the plural form "blues")
g) surprise (out of the blue)
h) rarity (once in a blue moon)
i) excellence (blue ribbon)
j) dependability (blue chip stocks)
k) the working class (blue collar)
l) speed (talk a blue streak)

Both of the following quotations describe the same woman, with the same possessions and features; but she is described by two different observers with such connotative language that the reader may think she is two different people.

Compare the details in paragraph (a) with the parallel details in (b); analyze their connotations. Paragraph (a) is from Dickens's *Hard Times*, paragraph (b) is a paraphrase done as an exercise.

(a) It was an old woman, tall and shapely still, though withered by time, on whom his eyes fell when he stopped and turned. She was very cleanly and plainly dressed, had country mud upon her shoes, and was newly come from a journey. The flutter of her manner, in the unwonted noise of the streets; the spare shawl carried unfolded on her arm; the heavy umbrella, and little basket; the loose long-fingered gloves, to which her hands were unused; all bespoke an old woman from the country, in her plain holiday clothes, come into Coketown on an expedition of rare occurrence.

(b) It was an old hag, lanky but well-fed though desiccated with age, on whom his eyes fell when he stopped and turned. She was clad in cheap, bleached muslin, her shoes were caked with mud, and she had obviously just sneaked into town. The shabbiness of her manner in contrast to the sophisticated city; the superfluous shawl, dangling sloppily from her arm; the ridiculously large umbrella; the fatuously tiny basket; the pretentious gloves that didn't fit her — all betrayed a shabby crone making a foray into the city.

O. Swing, 1972   **Kelly Wise**

Exercises

A. In the paragraph below from John Steinbeck's *The Grapes of Wrath*, numbers inside parentheses indicate where connotative words have been removed. Select from the choices of words below the more appropriately connotative word for each parenthesis, and be prepared to justify your choice. No word choice is supplied for numbers 7 and 8; here you should find your own words which should fit with the mood of the paragraph.

Flies struck the screen with little bumps and (1) away. The compressor (2) for a time and then stopped. On 66 the traffic (3) by, trucks and (4) streamlined cars and jalopies, and they went by with a (5) whiz. Mae took down the plates and (6) the pie crust into a (7). She found her damp cloth and wiped the counter with circular sweeps. And her eyes were on the highway, where life (8) by.

1. droned, flew, sped
2. howled, ran, chugged
3. drove, raced, whizzed
4. fine, expensive, modern
5. loud, violent, vicious
6. dropped, scraped, put

B. Explain briefly your reasons for choosing particular words in answer to the questions below:

1. If you had just completed a delicate political deal which of the following terms would you wish were applied to you?

   cunning   sly
   sneaky   astute
   crafty   tricky
   artful

2. Which word appears to you to suggest the most urgency?

   imperative   compelling
   pressing   critical
   crucial

3. Which of the following connotes the *least* value for your money?

   expensive   exorbitant
   costly   extravagant
   high-priced

4. By which term do you think your English teacher would prefer to be known?

teacher	instructor
educator	pedagogue

C. Here is a writing assignment in three parts: read all parts before beginning.

   1. Using connotative language, write a derogatory or satiric characterization of a person, real or imaginary. Underline at least five connotative words; do not go so far as to use invective or hysterical language. Focus on small details.

   2. Characterize the same person, reducing the connotative language to neutral terms, as devoid of emotion as possible. Challenge: to avoid dullness.

   3. Characterize the same person, favorably, using connotative language that is complimentary. Try to use details that are parallel to the details in the first paragraph.

Figurative Language

Figurative language achieves a meaning or effect different from literal statement. Most figures of speech compare, explicitly or implicitly, two basically different things that share a common characteristic.

I. **Figures**

    A. **Simile** is an explicit comparison between two things that are literally quite different, a comparison using a word such as "like" or "as."

        Your brother ran like a gazelle. (but not "Your brother looks like you" — a comparison, not a simile. Why?)

        Her tenderness hovered over him like a flutter of wings. (Joseph Conrad, *Lord Jim*)

    B. **Metaphor** compares two things that are literally quite unlike, without a comparison word.

        For dust thou art, and unto dust shalt thou return. (Genesis, 3:19)

        Exhilaration is the Breeze
        That lifts us from the ground (Emily Dickinson)

        I suppose I could have redrawn this letter — rubbed out an eye, shortened a nose — so my portrait should not show me quite so clearly a fool (though unyoung, yet a young fool!), but a letter is no longer genuine when it abandons the moment that made it, when it no longer moves toward its recipient as though hurled by feeling from a bow. (William H. Gass, "A Letter To The Editor")

Proverbs are frequently rich in metaphor. Explain the metaphors in the following proverbs:

    No cross, no crown.

    One man's meat is another man's poison.

    I know which way the wind blows.

    We never know the worth of water till the well is dry.

    Hunger is the best sauce.

    Nothing but a handful of dust will fill the eye of man.

There are many types of metaphors besides the simple metaphor just defined.

C. Metonymy is the use of a closely related image for the idea:

> The White House has announced that . . . (a building represents the President or one of his aides)

> The Crown denies that . . . (ceremonial device worn by the king or the queen represents that ruler)

or the use of a significant, relevant part for the whole thing, sometimes called **Synecdoche:**

> All hands on deck.

> Do you have any wheels tonight?

D. Personification is the attribution of human characteristics to non-human (sometimes abstract) things. For example, Keats calls Autumn "Close bosom-friend of the maturing sun," and later says:

> Sometimes whoever seeks abroad may find
> Thee sitting careless on a granary floor,
> Thy hair soft-lifted by the winnowing wind.

E. Implicit Metaphor, a more subtle type of metaphor, avoids the construction "A is B"; instead it says, "A has the following strange qualities (implied: the qualities belong to B)."

"Suspicion slithered quietly into the room and coiled itself, ready to strike at the slightest provocation" contains an implicit metaphor. Nowhere in the sentence does the writer actually state "Suspicion is a snake," but he implies that and a good deal more.

What is the implicit metaphor in these opening four lines of Shakespeare's Sonnet 73?

> That time of year thou mayest in me behold
> When yellow leaves, or none, or few, do hang
> Upon those boughs which shake against the cold,
> Bare ruined choirs, where late the sweet birds sang.

F. An **Extended Metaphor** is a metaphor developed consistently and carefully throughout the paragraph or essay. It can be a powerful unifying device.

Kenneth Grahame uses extended metaphor in the following paragraph from *The Wind in the Willows:*

Nature's Grand Hotel has its Season, like the others. As the guests one by one pack, pay, and depart, and the seats at the *table-d'hote** shrink pitifully at each succeeding meal; as suites of rooms are closed, carpets taken up, and waiters sent away; those boarders who are staying on, *en pension,*** until the next year's full reopening, cannot help being somewhat affected by all these flittings and farewells, this eager discussion of plans, routes, and fresh quarters, this daily shrinkage in the stream of comradeship. One gets unsettled, depressed, and inclined to be querulous. Why this craving for change? Why not stay on quietly here, like us, and be jolly? You don't know this hotel out of season, and what fun we have among ourselves, we fellows who remain and see the whole interesting year out. All very true, no doubt, the others always reply; we quite envy you — and some other year perhaps — but just now we have engagements — and there's the bus at the door — our time is up! So they depart, with a smile and a nod, and we miss them, and feel resentful. The Rat was a self-sufficing sort of animal, rooted to the land, and whoever went, he stayed; still he could not help noticing what was in the air, and feeling some of its influence in his bones.

II. Faulty Figures

A. Clichés. Once a metaphor becomes popular, especially in slang, it loses its force. Avoid all clichés.

He has piloted the ship of state through perilous seas into a safe harbor.

We thought he would pass all of his courses, but just as he reached the home stretch he ran out of gas.

B. Mixed Metaphors. Avoid using contradictory metaphors for the same idea.

His fiery response drowned all opposition.

This virgin forest, pregnant with natural wealth, is the only portion of the state where the hand of man has not set foot.

*table-d'hote: meal served to all guests at a stated hour and fixed price; literally, the "host's table"
**en pension: as lodgers

P. Mr. and Mrs. Steve Mills, Pilgrim Theatre, 1974   **Roswell Angier**

A variation of this fault is the illogical development of a metaphor. Here is an editorial in the *New York Times*, 6 July 1972. Note the metaphors that are underlined.

Another Lithuanian has burned himself to death to protest Soviet occupation of his country, it is reported from Moscow. This is the latest sobering reminder of the <u>wave</u> of discontent that has <u>broken out</u> this year in the tiny Baltic country whose independence, along with that of her two neighbors, was <u>extinguished</u> by Stalin more than three decades ago as one of the side <u>dividends</u> of the Soviet-Nazi pact. It is a meaure of the desperation many Lithuanians feel that three in the last several weeks have chosen self-immolation as means of calling world attention to their plight.

The Catholic religion and Lithuanian nationalism are so intertwined that there is no point in debating whether it is religious or national oppression that is at the root of the current discontent. Rather, the protest petitions and other appeals for help that have been smuggled out of Lithuania suggest that Lithuanians believe that Moscow wishes to extirpate both the Catholic religion and Lithuanian language and culture. The purpose would of course be forcibly to assimilate the tiny Lithuanian nation into the vast sea of Russians — a practice known in czarist days simply as "russification."

What is most remarkable about the recent outburst of overt Lithuanian resistance is the role of the young, of those who were born and grew up under Soviet rule and have no memories of an independent Lithuanian state. The first Lithuanian to burn himself alive was a young worker, Roman Kalanta. His personal sacrifice in May ignited several days of massive riots during which thousands of young Lithuanians fought the police and troops in the streets of Kaunas.

So long as the Lithuanians protest alone, of course, Moscow has more than enough force to repress their discontent. But there is every reason to suppose that there is similar nationalist passion in the Ukraine, Georgia, Azerbaijan, Uzbekistan, Kazakhstan and other non-Russian republics, not to mention the other two Baltic states of Latvia and Estonia. If the non-Russian minorities were ever able to integrate their activities and present a united front against russification, Moscow would have a major challenge on its hands.

Exercises

A. 1. Making use of **simile**, describe the following:

   garbage cans   a cat's tail   fried onions
   egg shells   fresh paint   sunshine

   2. Making use of **personification**, describe the following:

   snow falling in the moonlight
   the fierce noonday sun
   sailing in a light storm
   a jet breaking the sound barrier

   3. Making use of a **metaphor**, describe the following:

   the smell of old newspaper
   the sound of tires on a snowy evening
   the taste of your favorite dessert
   the feel of a chamois (dry or wet) to your hand
   the sight of a falling star

   4. Express the following abstract concepts in terms of **metaphor**:

   envy   anticipation   love
   awe   defeat   charity

Some figurative examples:

Garbage cans lounging like derelicts in an alley. (simile)

Garbage cans open their rusty mouths to the rain. (personification)

Garbage cans, the cesspools of human wastefulness. (metaphor)

With the cavalier air of Robin Hood, he swung down from the balustrade and greeted the postman. (implicit simile)

Arms crossed over his chest like an ancient chieftain, he repeated his demands. (simile)

Suddenly he was engulfed by a sea of elation. Its waves . . . (metaphor)

B. Henry David Thoreau is justly admired as one of the outstanding prose stylists America has produced. In this paragraph from *Walden*, however, he has interwoven several different metaphors at the risk of confusing his readers. Make a list of the metaphors and then arrange them into at least three groups.

Let us spend one day as deliberately as Nature, and not be thrown off the track by every nutshell and mosquito's wing that falls on the rails. Let us rise early and fast, or break fast, gently and without perturbation; let company come and let company go, let the bells ring and the children cry — determined to make a day of it. Why should we knock under and go with the stream? Let us not be upset and overwhelmed in that terrible rapid and whirlpool called a dinner, situated in the meridian shallows. Weather this danger and you are safe, for the rest of the way is down hill. With unrelaxed nerves, with morning vigor, sail by it, looking another way, tied to the mast like Ulysses. If the engine whistles, let it whistle till it is hoarse for its pains. If the bell rings, why should we run? We will consider what kind of music they are like. Let us settle ourselves, and work and wedge our feet downward through the mud and slush of opinion, and prejudice, and tradition, and delusion, and appearance, that alluvion which covers the globe, through Paris and London, through New York and Boston and Concord, through church and state, through poetry and philosophy and religion, till we come to a hard bottom and rocks in place, which we can call *reality*, and say, This is, and no mistake; and then begin, having a *point d'appui*,* below freshet and frost and fire, a place where you might found a wall or a state, or set a lamppost safely, or perhaps a gauge, not a Nilometer, but a Realometer, that future ages might know how deep a freshet of shams and appearances had gathered from time to time.

C. Create sentences that include these phrases:

1. Beach girls, plump doves
2. Minutes lurching by like goats
3. Asphalt shining like molasses
4. Long sea fingers parting like beads
5. Slanting up like buried crosses
6. The slit of his searing eye
7. Shielding her wounded sensibility
8. Laughter, the dark cackle of a loon
9. Hucksters of early defeat
10. The chatter and gossip of finches
11. The lady's wit, a bludgeon
12. Gathered together like lint
13. The whorls of shells

point d'appui: a base (esp. for military action)

14. The whine of a sore and neglected piano
15. As innocent as a toddler peeking in a closet
16. Old pillows settling into sleep

D. Complete these constructions:

1. _____, like the sea, is layered like plankton.
2. The _____ of _____ hung like _____ in the air.
3. He hobbled down the corridor with the _____ of a _____.
4. The _____ of her _____ mind _____ upon him.
5. Milly had the _____ shoulders of a typist.
6. Insistent upon vindication, with _____ drumming in his mind, Sebastian took off on the motorcycle.
7. Marvin, a taxonomist of _____, delights in _____.
8. Her _____ questions probed the _____ of her argument and ground the _____ of the cunning secretary to _____.
9. Behind the _____ of her greeting lay _____, as palpable and kind as _____.
10. A smile like a _____ across her face.
11. Sunshine _____ among the swaying clouds.
12. His hands had the coarseness of _____.

E. Prepare to discuss in class the aptness of these figurative statements.

1. Those grades, a kite-burst of March wind, may come to the ground during June.
2. The red caesura of a barn.
3. Wind in an aged chimney, his voice murmured its complaint.
4. From topic to topic his thoughts hopped, like a dazed fly.
5. These sentences which we follow warily, as Alice after that rabbit.
6. Our own blood shaped by the smiles and whipcracks of our parents.
7. His resolve leaked energy like a ruptured pipe.
8. A cry the shape of a sparrow sprang from her lips.
9. The kitchen range sprouted rust like fur in the winter damp.
10. A row of exclamation points, his face a scarlet stubble, thrust up at us out of the rain.
11. Hands leering from sleeves like rumpled price tags.
12. He staked out the stages of his life like a victory garden.
13. The crowbar of his hate was inserted into the joints of their hypocrisy.
14. The arrow slipped into the humid air, arching high over the weathervane.

Q. Untitled, 1977   **Starr Ockenga**

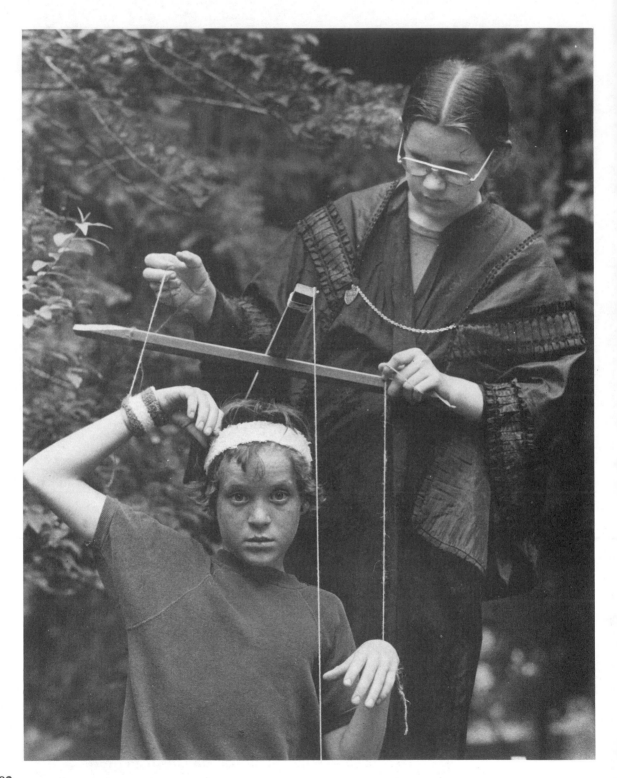

Style

Prose style can be as distinctive as human personality. Your favorite sports writer or novelist may have a particular style. For some pieces of writing he may vary this style. It is a simplification to say that a writer's style is classical or rich in metaphor or structured on the speech patterns of a Georgia Cracker. Style has many elements: structure, diction, logic, rhetoric, unity, clarity, concreteness, coherence. The list goes on and on. In the largest sense, style unites all of these.

Note the various styles in the passages that follow. Ask yourself how they differ. In some you will discover the use of poetic devices — reliance upon sound and rhythm. Some of these passages are like relief maps; they have quite different topographies.

1. Outside, the sun arises from its cradle in the treetops of the forest. Shadows of pines are dreams the sun shakes from its eyes. The sun arises. Gold glowing child, it steps into the sky and sends a birth-song slanting down gray dust streets and sleepy windows of the southern town. (Jean Toomer, *Cane*)

2. . . . Yes, the newspapers were right: snow was general all over Ireland. It was falling on every part of the dark central plain, on the treeless hills, falling softly upon the Bog of Allen and, farther westward, softly falling into the dark mutinous Shannon waves. It was falling, too, upon every part of the lonely churchyard on the hill where Michael Furey lay buried. It lay thickly drifted on the crooked crosses and headstones, on the spears of the little gate, on the barren thorns. His soul swooned slowly as he heard the snow falling faintly through the universe and faintly falling, like the descent of their last end, upon all the living and the dead. (James Joyce, "The Dead")

3. Frau Hutten flattened her hands at the edge of the table on either side of her plate and twiddled her fingers ever so slightly; her husband's tricks with his hands while talking made her nervous — they always had. Everybody looked as if he were listening to a sermon — a dull one. He was boring them to death again, she could feel it like vinegar in her veins. All in one vast drowning movement she remembered those many years when she had interposed herself, literally, bodily, between her husband and the seamy, grimy, mean, sordid, tiresome side of life that he simply could not endure. All those stupid details, all those endless errands, all that long war with the trickeries and the cheats and the slackness of the dishonest, the wayward, the greedy people of whom the entire working class from

top to bottom seemed to consist; she had dealt with them all, with that endless parade of them through the days of her life, without once disturbing her husband or asking for his help. The superiority of his mind, the importance of his profession, required that his energies and dignity be saved for the higher things of life, and so she had saved them. No one had ever seen the professor carry even the smallest parcel in his hand — not even a book to and from school. She carried everything, his books, paper parcels, suitcases, string bags, and even pushed a market cart before her like a baby carriage. She had done it with pride and love, for everybody who saw her knew that her husband was a distinguished professor and that she was a good devoted wife who did everything well. "The ideal German wife," she had been called by persons she had reason to trust and respect. (Katherine Anne Porter, *Ship of Fools*)

4. Having gathered together the fevers, the conquests, the passions, having pulled in the sails of my everrestless, everwandering ships of dreams . . . having garnered, collected, called back from the Tibetan desert my ever-roaming soul, having rescued my spirit from the webs of the past, from the stranglehold of responsibility for the lives of others, having cured myself of the drugs of romanticism, surrendered the impossible dreams, and called back an exhausted Don Quixote, I close the window, and the door, and open the diary once more. (Anais Nin, *The Diary of Anais Nin*)

5. The people of England will not ape the fashions they have never tried, nor go back to those which they have found mischievous on trial. They look upon the legal hereditary succession of their crown as among their rights, not as among their wrongs; as a benefit, not as a grievance; as a security for their liberty, not as a badge of servitude. They look on the frame of their commonwealth, *such as it stands*, to be of inestimable value; and they conceive the undisturbed succession of the crown to be a pledge of the stability and perpetuity of all the other members of our constitution. (Edmund Burke, *Reflections on the Revolution in France*)

6. At any rate, despite all strainings and waverings, the ranks began to form behind the first rank, and a hollow square of young Mobilization monitors formed up ahead of the leading rank of notables in order to sweep like a plug or a piston along the bridge, thus keeping infiltrators from passing the flanks and destroying the front of the March, but the notables in consequence were shifted down from the forwardmost line to what was now no more than the third line, to

Mailer's disappointment, for he had been pleased to be in the front rank, in fact had fought doggedly to keep position there, anticipating at the end of the March a confrontation face to face with the eyes of soldiers guarding an entrance to the Pentagon, and thought if his head was to be busted this day, let it be before the eyes of America's TV viewers tonight. (Norman Mailer, *Armies of the Night*)

There are limits to style, however. When a writer's style calls attention to itself, meaning and communication may suffer. A particular problem is purple prose, writing that is elaborate, precious, and overly figurative. Often the writer uses archaic or foreign words, ornate phrases, and complex structures. It is easy to detect the unnaturalness of the writing; one can sometimes pare the sentences down to half of their length, especially by simplifying wordy phrasing. In the passage below, notice how even a great man of letters can be guilty of pretentious (if genuinely enthusiastic) brilliance and the excessive use of figurative language.

The Americans of all nations at any time upon the earth, have probably the fullest poetical nature. The United States themselves are essentially the greatest poem. In the history of the earth hitherto, the largest and most stirring appear tame and orderly to their ampler largeness and stir. Here at last is something in the doings of man that corresponds with the broadcast doings of the day and night. Here is action untied from strings, necessarily blind to particulars and details, magnificently moving in masses. Here is the hospitality which forever indicates heroes. Here the performance, disdaining the trivial, unapproach'd in the tremendous audacity of its crowds and groupings, and the push of its perspective, spreads with crampless and flowing breadth, and showers its profilic and splendid extravagance. One sees it must indeed own the riches of the summer and winter, and need never be bankrupt while corn grows from the ground, or the orchards drop apples, or the bays contain fish, or men beget children upon women. (Walt Whitman, *Leaves of Grass*)

Analyze in a paragraph the specific differences in style between the two quotations.

(a) The Mole hurried along. He anticipated the moment when he would be at home again. He wanted to be among the things that he knew and liked. The Mole saw clearly that he was an animal of the tilled field. He belonged to the hedgerow. He was linked to the ploughed furrow. He was a native of the frequented pasture. He liked the lane where creatures gathered in the evening. He missed the cultivated garden-plot.

(b) As he hurried along, eagerly anticipating the moment when he would be at home again among the things he knew and liked, the Mole saw clearly that he was an animal of the tilled field and hedgerow, linked to the ploughed furrow, the frequented pasture, the lane of evening lingerings, the cultivated garden-plot. (Kenneth Grahame, *The Wind in the Willows*)

V.
Contemporary Usage

Avoiding Common Errors

Punctuation

Four Fundamental Spelling Rules

Quotations

Footnotes and Bibliography

The Business Letter

Avoiding Common Errors

1. *Its* (possessive) and *It's* (contraction for *it is*)

   Its splendor shone like a rainbow.

   "It's mine," he said.

2. *To* (preposition) and *Too* (adverb)

   To betray a friend is to betray yourself.

   Too often what we read in the press is a distortion of fact.

3. *Who, That, Which*

   He is one who should diet.

   It was our nationality that so irritated the customs officer.

   Beyond the cove, which lay in slumbrous sun, a yawl canted slowly towards the horizon.

4. Use *often*, not *oftentimes*; *different from*, not *different than*; *could have*, not *could of*

5. Adjectives — *good*   Adverbs — *well*
                  real   *really*

   He swims well for his age.

   I felt really ill after the party.

6. Hyphenate words

   used as a single adjective before a noun: *far-sighted* decision, *ill-conceived* project, *old-fashioned* person

   used in compound numbers, 21 to 99: *twenty-five, forty-four, seventy-nine*

   used with the prefix *self* (exception — *selfless*): *self-contained, self-conscious, self-confidence*

7. Use a semicolon before words like *however, nevertheless, therefore,* and *thus* if they introduce a clause in the second half of the sentence.

   The garden is dry; however, after some cultivating and a thorough sprinkling, those drooping plants should again look spry.

   I have accepted your proposal; therefore, a check will be forthcoming.

8. In comparisons *like* is a preposition and *as* is a subordinating conjunction.

He ran like a sow with her litter beneath her.

Sally plays the violin as badly as she plays the cello.

9. In constructions using linking verbs, avoid using adverb clauses (*because . . ., when . . ., how . . .*) in place of noun clauses.

The reason he lost is *that* he was tired. (not *because* he was tired)

Do not use an adverb clause as the subject of the sentence.

(Wrong: *Just because it is raining* doesn't mean the game is canceled.)

(Correct: Rain does not necessarily cancel the game.)

10. Avoid the crutch of weak, vague diction when you can be more specific. Particularly lazy words — *aspect, phase, factor, thing, situation.*

Particularly lazy constructions —

the fact that

as to

as far as . . . is concerned

in terms of

being that

all adverbs made from a noun with the suffix -*wise* (*weatherwise, moneywise, healthwise*)

11. Words commonly confused:

accept	receive (verb)
except	excluding (preposition)
advise	urge (verb)
advice	counsel (noun)
affect	to influence (verb)
effect	end, result (noun)
effect	to produce (verb)
almost	nearly
most	(a superlative; as a colloquial contraction for *almost* it should be avoided, as in "Most everybody from the office went to the party.")

coarse	rough (adjective)
course	direction (noun)
compliment	praise (noun)
compliment	to praise (verb)
complement	to complete (verb)
conscience	moral sense (noun)
conscious	aware (adjective)
council	group (noun)
counsel	advice (noun)
counsel	to advise (verb)
desert	wasteland (noun)
dessert	food (noun)
desert	abandon (verb)
imply	suggest
infer	assume, draw from
insinuate	suggest (something negative)
later	succeeding at another time
latter	second of two
lead	metal (noun)
lead	conduct (verb)
led	conducted (past participle of verb *lead*)
lend	give out (verb)
loan	temporary grant (noun)
principal	sum of money that does not include interest
principal	school administrator (noun)
principal	foremost (adjective)
principle	basic doctrine (noun)
prophesy	to predict (verb)
prophecy	prediction (noun)
they're	they are (contraction)
their	possessive (adjective)
there	in that place (adverb)
who's	who is (contraction)
whose	possessive
you're	you are (contraction)
your	possessive

1. **Sentence Fragment:** a phrase or subordinate clause punctuated as a full sentence. (Sometimes writers use fragments intentionally for emphasis.)

   The cat climbing in the window.

   The engineer who hoped that this time the experiment would work.

Correction: Be sure there is a verb (not just a participle) in the sentence. Perhaps the fragment should be joined to the preceding or following sentence.

   The cat was climbing in the window.

   The director encouraged the engineer, who hoped that this time the experiment would work.

2. **Run-on Sentence:** two main clauses, or sentences, joined with no punctuation (also known as a fused sentence) or with only a comma (also known as a comma splice).

   Geraniums are hardy flowers they can grow almost anywhere.

   Marsha knew perfectly well what the problem was, she didn't correct it, though.

Correction: Use either a comma and a coordinating conjunction, or simply a semicolon to join the two main clauses.

   Geraniums are hardy flowers; they can grow almost anywhere.

   Marsha knew perfectly well what the problem was, but she didn't correct it.

3. **Misplaced Modifier:** a modifying word, phrase, or clause placed somewhere in the sentence other than next to the element it is meant to modify.

   We bought the firecrackers from a Tennessee store, which cost $4.50.

   Bill uses tennis balls for practice with no fuzz on them.

   I only ate one egg for breakfast.

Correction: Move the modifier next to the element it is to modify.

   We bought the firecrackers, which cost $4.50, from a Tennessee store.

   For practice, Bill uses tennis balls with no fuzz on them.

   I ate only one egg for breakfast.

4. **Dangling Modifier:** a modifier that has nothing specific in the sentence to modify.

> Stopping to consider where their next meal is coming from, their faces grow sadder and their frowns become larger.

> Driving through the valley, the trees were breathtakingly beautiful.

Correction: Either supply a noun for the modifier to modify or rewrite the sentence to turn the phrase into a clause.

> As they consider where their next meal is coming from, their faces grow sadder and their frowns become larger.

> Driving through the valley, we found the trees breathtakingly beautiful.

5. **Faulty Agreement:** subjects and verbs that do not agree in number, or pronouns that do not agree with their antecedents in number.

> The performance of the madrigals precede the intermission.

> The sign lasted for about two weeks until it just fell down or someone borrowed the tack for their own notice.

> Neither my grandparents nor Teddy are going to the fair.

Correction: Match verbs with subjects, pronouns with antecedents; singular with singular, plural with plural. The verb agrees with the nearest noun in *either . . . or . . .* and *neither . . . nor . . .* constructions.

> The performance of the madrigals precedes the intermission.

> The sign lasted for about two weeks until it just fell down or someone borrowed the tack for his own notice.

> Neither my grandparents nor Teddy is going to the fair.

6. **Faulty Parallelism:** repeated constructions that are not equivalent in syntax or form.

> Superman fought for truth, justice, and keeping crime out of Metropolis.

> Water-skiing is much safer than to ski on snow.

> The fugitive sprinted for the fence; he grasped at the spikes, swung himself over; he was last seen diving into the moat.

Correction: For balance, use similar elements in repeated constructions; follow a word with a word, a phrase with a phrase, a clause with a clause.

Superman fought for truth, justice, and law in Metropolis.

Water-skiing is much safer than snow-skiing.

The fugitive sprinted for the fence, grasped at the spikes, swung himself over, and dived into the moat.

7. **Redundancy:** unintentional repetition.

The people whom I disagree with fall under the headings of people who are hypocritical and "two-faced."

Correction: Be sure not to say the same thing twice.

The people whom I disagree with are hypocritical.

8. **Faulty Diction:** the wrong word used in a given context.

Your speech infers that America is headed for bankruptcy.

Correction: Find the proper word.

Your speech implies that America is headed for bankruptcy.

9. **Inconsistent Person:** mixing first, second, and third person pronouns.

If one is genuinely interested in constructive hobbies, sewing offers great dividends in satisfaction and economy; you should try it.

Correction: Use the same person throughout a sentence, paragraph, or composition.

If you are genuinely interested in constructive hobbies, sewing offers great dividends in satisfaction and economy; you should try it.

10. **Incorrect Pronoun Case:** use of a pronoun in a case inappropriate to its function in the sentence.

Franklin Pierce is the President who I know least about.

Willy Ripley, whom everyone thinks is my best friend, has let me down badly more than once.

They live farther from Nelsonville than us.

Everyone passed the exam but I.

S. Embudo Pass, New Mexico, 1974   Cary Wasserman

Correction: Determine the function of the pronoun in its own clause or phrase and use the appropriate form. Sometimes it is helpful to add words that clarify the meaning of the sentence.

Franklin Pierce is the President whom I know least about. (*whom* is object of *I know*)

Willy Ripley, who everyone thinks is my best friend, has let me down badly more than once. (*who* is subject of *is my best friend*)

They live farther from Nelsonville than we. (verb *do* is understood)

Everyone passed the exam but me. (*me* is object of *but*)

11. **Vague Pronoun Reference:** pronouns (especially *this* and *which*) without specific antecedents or with remote antecedents.

The teacher sat on the tack, which sent the class into an uproar.

This was one of the chief causes of the failure of the revolution.

Correction: Change the syntax of the sentence, often by eliminating relative clauses, or supply definite antecedents for the pronouns.

When the teacher sat on the tack, the class went into an uproar.

This inadequacy of supply lines was one of the chief causes of the failure of the revolution.

12. **Improper Emphasis:** important ideas in subordinate constructions, or ideas of unequal importance in coordinate structures.

The crowd hushed as the golfer poised over the ball, stroking it into the cup.

The jury returned to the courtroom and the defendant took his seat with obvious despair, and awaited the verdict.

Correction: Place important ideas in main clauses, lesser ideas in subordinate clauses or phrases; be sure ideas in coordinate constructions really are equal in importance.

As the crowd hushed, the golfer, poised over the ball, stroked it into the cup.

As the jury returned to the courtroom, the defendant took his seat with obvious despair, awaiting the verdict.

13. **Faulty Voice:** use of the passive voice when the active is more appropriate, or mixing active and passive voices.

> The little old man was smacked down by the mail truck.

> The boy stole a kiss from the girl, and was promptly slapped in the face.

Correction: Use the active voice (subject-verb-object) most of the time. Use passive voice when the agent of an action (normally the subject of the sentence) is unknown or unimportant. Don't mix active and passive voices in the same sentence.

> The mail truck smacked down the old man.

> The boy stole a kiss from the girl; she promptly slapped him in the face.

14. **Inconsistent Tense:** needless shifts among tenses or inappropriate sequence of tenses.

> The car hurtled madly down the freeway while the driver thinks only of the girl he met in San Jose.

> Freedom of religion had been newly established when Fox had arrived in the United States.

Correction: Once you have selected a tense, use it throughout unless you are looking back or forward in time.

> The car hurtled madly down the freeway while the driver thought only of the girl he had met in San Jose.

> Freedom of religion had been newly established when Fox arrived in the United States.

Exercise

Each of the following sentences contains one or more of the usage errors described above. List the error in each case and then correct the sentence.

1. Walking downtown, the bag of bottles fell out of his arms.

2. Neither Ned nor his parents knows the answer to that question.

3. Everyone should check their coat before going into the dance.

4. Integrity, being generous, and forthrightness — these are the attributes we seek in a leader.

5. The illogic of your false argument is obvious: you mistake effects for causes.

6. I'll loan you $2000 to help reduce the principle on your mortgage.

7. After the widow passed away, the farm was sold by her heirs, they also sold her two-story in town.

8. He missed the play his sister forgot to tell him about it.

9. Having been jolted out of his indolence, having been lectured to by his parents, having once again renewed his pledge to his girlfriend, Ralph's determination to get a job.

10. The bill only guaranteed protection for the rich.

11. The affect of your decision is to undermine our party and assure victory for your opponent.

12. A person is bound to feel resentment when your car is vandalized.

13. His aunt is the woman standing next to the flag pole with the red hat.

14. The president of the firm announced that it was bankrupt, which was no surprise to anyone.

15. Mr. Carver totaled his car and he bled to death before reaching the hospital.

16. The reward of $5 was spent by the boys for candy.

17. Robert Frost is the poet who New Englanders most admire.

18. Either you or I are mistaken.

19. A good race was run by Jake.

20. A sister who has just hit her little brother and feels important after her act of superiority.

21. His life wasn't lived for himself it was for God and humanity.

22. Plus the long, slow, humble, and humiliating walk to congratulate the victors and head for the showers.

23. Similar to the telescope, the microscope has an uncertain origin lost in improbable legends of the Middle Ages which, if true, could have been the ancestor of the first magnifying glass.

24. One aspect of college that I enjoy very much is the fact that I have more freedom.

25. Just because the book is short doesn't mean its easy to read.

26. I think that Fritz could of won the election if he had campaigned harder.

27. The trouble with the new interstate highway is that to many drivers ignore the speed limit.

28. If Reginald did indeed except the gift from his client, then it looks like he is guilty of unethical conduct.

29. Although the principle speaker was an authority on dessert life, most all of the audience fell asleep within five minutes.

30. The design of the book should compliment the text, however the cost of the book must not be prohibitive.

31. He is in trouble as far as money is concerned.

32. He is in trouble moneywise.

33. This year's school calendar is considerably different than last year's.

34. Its obvious to me that the computer requires it's rest period just as a human being.

35. Debbie had a bad conscious because the fire of her enthusiasm for chemistry wilted by the end of the second semester.

36. Latter in the book the author sarcastically infers that he himself should of been appointed Town Manager.

37. The Smith Institute is studying the effect of radiation on the liver in terms of it's red blood corpuscles.

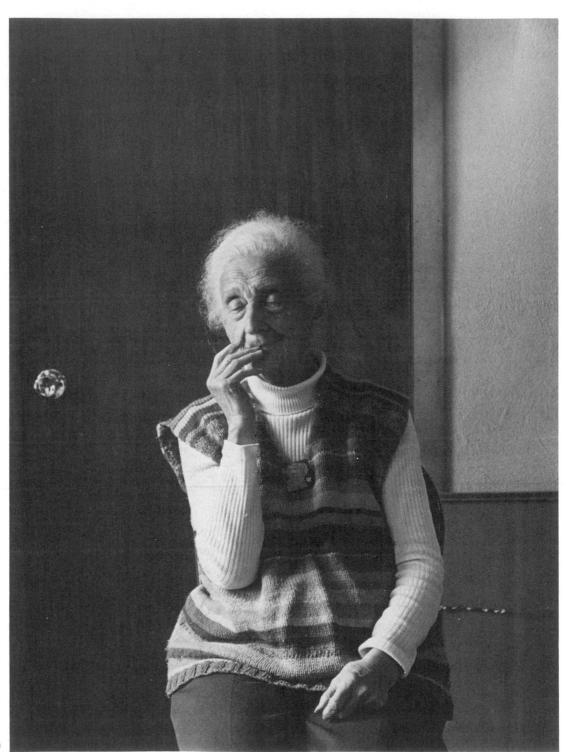

Punctuation

Nothing undermines your prose more rapidly than the apparent trifle of erroneous punctuation.

Like the alphabet itself, punctuation is conventional — agreed-upon like the rules of any game. And like those game rules, the conventions vary from age to age, from country to country. Consider, for example, how quotation marks vary from the "American" system to the 'British' system to the «German» system. This section merely describes current practice in America in the 1980s.

But punctuation rules are not whimsical. Since their common purpose is to help writers communicate with readers, the customs must make some sense and must be agreed upon by the majority of a culture. Thus we have symbols for different intensities of pause (comma, semi-colon, period), for raising the voice at the end of the sentence (question mark), for shouting (exclamation point), for speaking a quiet aside (parentheses) or an emphatic aside (dashes). So complicated is language, however, that even after centuries of developing the medium of English, we still have not devised symbols for every possible occasion — we have yet to agree, for example, on a single appropriate end mark for an exclamation that happens to be a question.

Comma

Because we ask the comma to serve so many functions, it is the punctuation mark that causes the most problems in student writing. Although the comma in a series looks exactly like the comma setting off an introductory adverbial clause, the two marks serve such different purposes that they could theoretically be represented by different symbols if we were to invent our language anew. Indeed, a more mathematically symbolic (and ponderous) language might well have six or seven symbols for our single comma.

Here are the four most important uses of the comma.

1. *To separate two main clauses that are joined by a coordinate conjunction.*

   It was getting towards evening, and the solemn stillness of the High Alps was broken only by the sound of rushing water or of falling rocks. (Edward Whymper, *Scrambles Amongst the Alps in the Years 1860-69*)

   She waved no plumes and rattled no sabers, but she seemed to be advancing at the head of a victorious army. (Louis Untermeyer, *From Another World*)

The omission of the coordinate conjunction requires a semicolon in place of the comma.

2. *To separate items in a series.* There are two kinds of series:

   a. Two or more coordinate adjectives:

      Adolph was uncomfortable because of the hot, dusty drive through town.

      Adolph was uncomfortable because of the hot, dusty, bumpy, slow drive through town.

   b. Three or more coordinate items:

      (single words) For breakfast Eric had ham, eggs, toast, and coffee.

      (prepositional phrases) The car skidded down the hill, across the grass, and into a ditch.

      (adverbial clauses) You must report to the supervisor if your machine breaks, if you feel ill, or if the alarm sounds.

3. *To set off certain introductory elements.*

   a. Introductory adverbial clause:

   When the rain stops, everyone must help roll up the canvas.

But omit the comma when the adverbial clause is not introductory:

   Everyone must help to roll up the canvas when the rain stops.

   b. Introductory verbal phrase:

   (gerund) By repairing the car himself, my brother saved almost one hundred dollars.

   (infinitive) To repair the car, my brother had to borrow the tools from Fred.

   (participle) Pedaling with all her might, Sarah sped past the only cyclist between her and the finish line.

As a general rule a mere prepositional phrase without a verbal should not have a comma after it:

   In the morning I prefer to have coffee instead of tea.

4. *To set off interrupters.*

   a. Parenthetical word or phrase:

   I am convinced, however, of his innocence.

   The tennis team, I am sorry to report, has lost every match of the season.

   b. Appositive:

   Mrs. Sutherland, my English teacher, plays trombone with a jazz group on weekends.

   c. Noun of direct address:

   I hope, Linda, that you remembered to turn off the water.

   d. Adjective clause that is not required for the identification of the noun it modifies, no matter how important the clause is to the rest of the sentence or the paragraph:

   George Washington, whose false teeth were made of wood, was never heard to complain about his severely restricted diet.

Omit the comma when the adjective clause is needed to identify the noun it modifies:

> The wretched pickpocket who stole my wallet is going to be sorry when I find him.

Occasionally — but only occasionally — a comma is required for clarity:

> To John, Franklin seemed to be the guilty party.

Overuse of the comma is just as bad as underpunctuation. Too much punctuation clutters the sentence, breaks the rhythm of the prose, and probably undermines the reader's confidence in the writer's skill. Do not use a comma unless there is a reason for using it.

Other uses of the comma.

The comma is used to distinguish adjacent numbers in dates:

> July 4, 1776

> (But no comma in the alternate form of 4 July 1776)

The comma is used to separate the major elements in an address when it is written run-on instead of in block form:

> The Independent School Press, 51 River Street, Wellesley Hills, Massachusetts 02181.

The words *yes* and *no* and mild interjections are set off from the rest of the sentence by a comma:

> Yes, I like chamber music.

> No, I do not own a tape recorder.

> Oh, I see your point now.

> Well, the decision is yours to make.

Period

The period is used at the end of a sentence that is a statement or an indirect question:

> The doctor asked if my elbow was still sore.

The period is also usually used after an abbreviation:

> Mr. Evans   etc.
>
> Dr. Lane   e.g.
>
> Mary Taylor, Ph.D.   i.e.

An alternative convention is growing that eliminates the period after some abbreviations:

Mr Evans

Dr Lane

e g

Simply be consistent: do not write "Mr." in one paragraph and "Mr" in another.

Three spaced periods, called ellipsis marks, indicate that some words are omitted from a quotation. Use a fourth period if the end of one or more sentences is involved in the omission.

Colon

A colon indicates a pause and voice drop before a list, definition, or explanation that usually is an appositive to a noun before the colon. (An appositive is a noun construction that identifies or describes an immediately preceding noun or pronoun: Adrian Glucose, *the only student in school who eats candy for breakfast*, is losing his teeth.)

I had to buy the following tools to build the shed: a hammer, a saw, a level, and a plane. (The list is in apposition to the noun *tools*.)

Note that there is no colon in the following sentence:

To build the shed, I had to buy a hammer, a saw, a level, and a plane. (There is no appositive.)

In America the colon is also used after the greeting in a formal business letter, and between hours and minutes when the time is written numerically:

Dear Mr. Irving: 8:31 a.m.

Dear Sir: 12:00 noon

Semicolon

In spite of its name, the semicolon is not so much a relative of the colon as of the comma in the first two comma rules.

1. The semicolon is used to separate two main clauses that are *not* joined by a coordinate conjunction:

    The young American Narcissus had looked at himself in the narrow rocky pools of New England and by the waters of the Mississippi; he also gazed at a darker image. (Constance Rourke, *American Humor*)

Probably the most common punctuation error is caused by the mistaken notion that a conjunctive adverb (*however, therefore, nevertheless*) is the same thing as a conjunction. The result is a comma splice, or two sentences posing as one.

    The rain showed no prospect of letting up, however the fireworks program was neither canceled nor postponed.

This error betrays the writer's ignorance of what a sentence is. A semicolon after "letting up" and a comma after "however" is one way of repairing the damage. A better way is subordinating one of the two clauses:

    Although the rain showed no prospect of letting up, the fireworks program was neither canceled nor postponed.

The semicolon is sometimes used to separate two main clauses even when they are joined by a coordinating conjunction. Frequently the reason for the semicolon is that there is significant punctuation (almost always commas) elsewhere in the sentence, and the writer wishes to show where the main division in the sentence occurs.

    They went over the house like ants, the house where they had never before got past the parlour; and they found they had been fooled all these years. (Willa Cather, *A Lost Lady*)

    A true poem contains the seed of wonder; but a bad poem, egg-fashion, stinks. (E.B. White, *One Man's Meat*)

2. The semicolon is used to set off items in a series when there is significant punctuation within the series:

    We had breakfast at Carlo's, a family restaurant near the hotel; lunch at a sidewalk cafe; and an elegant, two-hour dinner at the Snead's town house.

U. Stairway, 1972   **Kelly Wise**

Parentheses

Parentheses are used to set off a brief definition or a quiet interrupter of a sentence, like an "aside" in a play. An emphatic interrupter, on the other hand, is set off by dashes.

> The outdoor bowling game of Bocce (from the Italian for "ball") has been popular for almost two thousand years.

> The paradoxes of *Macbeth* are epitomized by the hero's observation "So foul and fair a day I have not seen" (I.iii.38).

Dash

The dash is used to set off an emphatic interrupter or (in place of a possible colon) an emphatic summary:

> The very name of Plautus meant belly laughs, charm, wit, song — in a word, entertainment. (Erich Segal, *Plautus: Three Comedies*)

> We begin to have the odd feeling that we are watching a play within a play or — as the levels of deception multiply — a play within a play within a play. (Alvin B. Kernan, *Ben Johnson: "Volpone"*)

Note that in Kernan's sentence the interrupter could have been set off several different ways: by parentheses, commas, or dashes. Each of the three choices can be justified. Since the author has chosen dashes, he wishes us to read the interrupter emphatically instead of as a quiet aside.

Although interrupters have an integral role in the patterns of English sentences, using an abundance of dashes and parentheses in your writing creates a staccato or hiccup effect which ruins the flow of your sentences. Use interrupters sparingly.

The average typewriter does not have a dash on the keyboard. The current convention for typing a dash is to skip a space, type two consecutive hyphens, and skip another space before the next word -- like that. As a mark of punctuation the dash *separates*. The hyphen is really a mark of spelling rather than of punctuation. It *joins*.

Observe that parentheses should be used in pairs, i.e., both an open parenthesis and a close parenthesis (like this). Although dashes usually occur in pairs also, if the interrupter comes at the end of the sentence, as in Erich Segal's sentence above, the second dash is displaced by the final period — like this.

Brackets

Brackets are used to explain or clarify something in a quotation, without requiring you to close the quotation marks and open them again. The most frequent use is to identify a noun or pronoun in a quotation.

> In his introductory essay Martin Battestin claims "But Parson Adams is the supreme achievement of the novel [*Joseph Andrews*], the best character that Fielding ever created and among the most memorable in any literature."

> The critic Clement Eliot is convinced that "The impact of the Impressionist painters on her [Virginia Woolf's] novels has yet to be fully studied and evaluated."

Since most typewriters do not have square brackets, the writer usually inserts them with a pen.

Question Mark

The question mark is used at the end of a direct question:

> Her lawyer asked me, "Where were you on last December 1?"

Unless the entire sentence is a question, a period is used at the end of an indirect question:

> Her lawyer asked me where I was on last December 1.

> Did her lawyer ask you where you were on last December 1?

Exclamation Point

The exclamation point is used at the end of an emotional or vehement sentence, phrase, or word:

> "Get out! I hate you!" screamed the spoiled brat at his tearful mother.

Some students infer that if one exclamation point shows emotion, three or five exclamation points must show three or five times as much emotion. Since the ultimate effect of such a practice is not so much a strengthening of five exclamation points as it is a weakening of the single mark, mature writers scrupulously avoid multiple exclamation points.

Quotation Marks

Quotation marks set off direct quotations and titles of short works like poems or short stories.

Quotation marks cause almost as much vexation as the comma does to the student writer, probably for several reasons: British and American customs differ, and we read books from both countries; there is a vast number of variations with endmarks; and custom rather than logic governs much of the usage.

American printers use "double" quotation marks for quotations, and 'single' marks for quotations-within-quotations. British printers reverse the process, beginning with 'single' quotation marks (or 'inverted commas').

In general, punctuation at the end of a quotation is placed inside the quotation marks if it belongs to the quotation, and outside the marks if it is not part of the quotation. But there are some conflicts and exceptions.

a) If the quotation (as opposed to your sentence surrounding the quotation) requires a question mark or an exclamation point, use that mark inside the quotation marks — it takes precedence over the mark for your own sentence:

Clem inquired, "Where are we going to play poker tonight?"

Observe that there is no period at the end, even though the words governing the quotation compose a declarative sentence. Two end marks (?".) are not used. If you reverse the two clauses, both the question mark and the period have their proper places:

"Where are we going to play poker tonight?" inquired Clem.

This time the comma has been displaced by the question mark. One problem on which we have no firm agreement yet is what to do with the following sentence:

"Where are we going to play poker tonight?" Clem inquired.

The omission of the comma has been the rule until the last few years. But because the capital *C* of *Clem* looks like the beginning of a new sentence, the reader tends to end the sentence at the question mark. And so some printers and publications allow the additional comma (once absolutely forbidden) to avoid ambiguity:

"Where are we going to play poker tonight?", Clem inquired.

b) If *your* sentence (not the quotation) requires either a period or a comma at the end of the quotation, place the period or comma inside the quotation marks. This custom may seem illogical, but it is convenient.

"I love poker," Clem confessed.

In the original statement by Clem there was a period where the comma now is. Convention allows you to convert that period to a comma for use in your sentence.

Alex does not believe that life "is a tale told by an idiot, full of sound and fury."

In the original *Macbeth* quotation the comma after *fury* has been displaced by the period required for the writer's sentence. (British custom however, more logically places the new period or comma outside the quotation marks.)

c) If your sentence requires a colon or a semicolon at the end of a quotation, place that punctuation outside the quotation marks:

Maybe you believe that life is "full of sound and fury"; I don't.

As you can see from the last two examples, quotation marks are used for more than dialogue. Besides indicating the titles of short works, they are also used for quoting from other works that are not dialogue. A problem now arises for the assiduous student who slavishly learned the rule in elementary school that "Words governing a quotation are set off by a comma" — for example, the comma in the sentence

Clem inquired, "Where are we going to play poker tonight?"

The rule holds only for conversation or dialogue quotations. When a quotation fits the flow of your sentence, no commas should be added:

Macbeth's "sound and fury" has little relevance for the speaker in Eliot's "The Love Song of J. Alfred Prufrock."

Some students mechanically add a comma wherever they see quotation marks; the addition of any commas to the above sentence would chop it up unmercifully.

Avoid the lazy device of using quotation marks to indicate slang, clichés, sarcasm, or careless diction. In such instances the quotation marks are a cheap appeal to the reader not to be excessively critical; the effect is just the opposite. You are drawing attention to your weak vocabulary. Spend a few minutes more to come up with the precise words you need.

Underlining (to indicate *italics*)

Since neither handwriting nor the average typewriter allows the writer to shift from normal script or type to *italics*, convention dictates the use of underlining to indicate italics.

Italics are used for titles of books, movies, magazines, newspapers (except by the newspapers themselves, ironically), record albums, art works, and ships. Italics also signify words or letters that are used out of context:

> Because she fills her sentences with too many *and*'s, her prose is monotonous. (On your typewriter, *and*'s would be typed and's.)
>
> Steve has the irritating habit of neglecting to cross his *t*'s. (Type t's.)

Indicate the title of a shorter work (like a poem, short story, or essay) by quotation marks; indicate the title of a larger work by italics:

> Robert Lowell's poem "Memories of West Street and Lepke" can be found in Donald Hall's Penguin anthology Contemporary American Poetry.

Apostrophe

Although more strictly a mark of spelling rather than of punctuation, the apostrophe is conveniently linked with punctuation on our typewriters and in our minds.

The apostrophe is used to indicate

a) possessive of all nouns and a few pronouns

b) plural of lower case letters

c) contraction

To indicate the possessive case, add an apostrophe and an *s* to all singular nouns except those ending in an *s* sound that cannot conveniently or smoothly take the extra *s* syllable. Thus,

Mr. Hearn's book

Marian Jones's car

but

Ulysses' journey

Aristophanes' comedies.

Plural nouns ending in *s* take only an apostrophe for the possessive:

cars' engines

ladies' apparel

A few nouns sound clumsy in the possessive case; in those instances, resort to the "of . . ." construction:

the doors of the firehouse (not "the firehouse's doors")

the covers of the books (preferred to "the books' covers")

Other plurals behave like singular nouns:

women's rights

data's importance

Most pronouns do not use an apostrophe in the possessive (its, hers, his, ours, my, mine, your, yours, whose), but only in contractions (*it's = it is, who's = who is*). A few pronouns, however, behave like nouns (someone's, anybody's, another's).

Plurals of lower case letters. Form the plurals of numbers and of capital letters by adding just an *s* with no apostrophe if the construction creates no ambiguity:

The 1970s were troublesome times.

Cross out all four of the 2s in the equation.

All the *F*s on the page were mistakenly italicized.

But to avoid confusion, add an apostrophe and an *s* to form the plurals of all lower case letters and a few capitals (especially *I* and *A*):

All of the *s*'s and *c*'s should sound alike in your rhyme scheme.

The *I*'s and *A*'s were not italicized.

Without the apostrophe, *Is* looks like the verb *is*, *As* like the conjunction *as*.

Contractions. The apostrophe indicates one or more missing letters in a contraction: don't (do not), it's (it is), you're (you are), haven't (have not). The only major problem here is the frequent confusion of *its* and *it's*, and by analogy the habit some students have of creating erroneous and meaningless forms like *her's* or *its'*.

A final word. Although most students are at least subconsciously aware of the following convention, it must nevertheless be stated for the benefit of those who may err: except for open quotation marks, open parentheses or brackets, and occasionally a dash, punctuation never is placed at the beginning of a line.

Exercise

Correct the punctuation in the following sentences and give the reason for each correction.

1. I have never had to memorize the To be or not to be soliloquy from Hamlet, therefore I cannot easily recognize allusions to the speech.

2. Mr. Albatross my ornithology teacher believes that there is only one subject worth studying in college; birds.

3. Mr. Albatrosses textbook A Complete Guide to American Birds published by the Greenview Press in Ballardvale is worth reading, however the price is outrageously high, fifty dollars.

4. In the long run, I do not think that, "Mending Wall," should be removed from our poetry syllabus, it is too important to miss.

5. Exactly what was Herbs tone of voice when he asked where is my wife.

6. His first chapter covers: robins, swallows, cardinals, and catbirds.

Four Fundamental Spelling Rules

    1. *ie* rule
    2. final consonant rule
    3. final silent *e* rule
    4. final *y* rule

In spite of the difficulties of English spelling, many words are conveniently governed by simple rules.

1. *ie* Rule. Place *i* before *e* except after *c*, or pronounced like an *a*, as in *neighbor* or *weigh*.

regular	after c	sounds like "a"
thief	receive	reign
priest	perceive	vein
friend	conceit	feign
besiege	ceiling	
chief		
fiend		

This contrived sentence contains most common exceptions:

Neither leisured foreigner seized the weird height for a forfeit.

2. Final Consonant Rule.
    If a word (a) is accented on the final syllable,
             (b) ends in a single consonant, and
             (c) is preceded by a single vowel,
double that final consonant before adding a suffix that begins with a vowel.

occur   (add -ence) _____ occurrence
hop   (add -ing) _____ hopping
fit   (add -ed) _____ fitted
BUT benefit (add -ed) _____ benefited
                  (accent not on final syllable)
succeed   (add -ed) _____ succeeded
                  (preceded by *two* vowels)
refer   (add -ed) _____ referred
but refer (add -ence) _____ reference
                  (accent shifts from last syllable)

3. Final Silent *e* Rule. Drop the final silent *e* before a suffix beginning with a vowel.

Retain the final silent *e* before a suffix beginning with a consonant.

vowel suffix

write	(add -ing)	_____	writing
refuse	(add -al)	_____	refusal
like	(add -able)	_____	likable

consonant suffix

nine	(add -ty)	_____	ninety
manage	(add -ment)	_____	management
entire	(add -ly)	_____	entirely

Exception: Retain the *e* before *o* and *a* suffixes to preserve the soft sound of *c* or *g*.

| courage | (add -ous) | _____ | courageous |
| notice | (add -able) | _____ | noticeable |

Some other exceptions: truly, wholly, awful, argument, ninth.

4. Final *y* Rule. If a final *y* is preceded by a consonant, change the *y* to *i* before adding the suffix (except the suffix -*ing*).

    If the *y* is preceded by a vowel, retain the *y* before a suffix.

simply	(add -fy)	_____	simplify
friendly	(add -ness)	_____	friendliness
lady	(add -es)	_____	ladies
lonely	(add -ness)	_____	loneliness
study	(add -es)	_____	studies
defy	(add -ance)	_____	defiance
cry	(add -ing)	_____	crying
relay	(add -ing)	_____	relaying
monkey	(add -s)	_____	monkeys
modify	(add -ing)	_____	modifying
study	(add -ing)	_____	studying
repay	(add -ment)	_____	repayment

Quotations

Using a quotation will often be the most effective way to prove your point. It is important, therefore, to know how to incorporate quotations into your writing.

1. *A word or brief phrase.* Sometimes you will wish to quote only a word or a phrase from a sentence. To do this you need only place that word or phrase in quotation marks to indicate that "thy words be few" (Ecclesiastes 5:2).

2. *A sentence or a major portion of one.* Separate from your own prose a quoted sentence (or a major portion of one) by the usual quotation marks. Emerson wrote, "Next to the originator of a good sentence is the first quoter of it."

3. *Words omitted in the middle of a quotation.* To indicate that some of the passage has been omitted, simply insert ellipsis marks (. . .). Samuel Johnson maintained, "Every quotation contributes something to the stability . . . of the language." Use a fourth period if the end of one or more sentences occurs in the omitted material.

4. *Poetry and longer prose within your text.* Set off from your own prose all poetry of two or more lines, and longer prose quotations (standards vary, but the usual guidelines are a passage of two or more sentences that run more than three typewritten lines) by centering them on the page (i.e., indented several spaces from your own margin), single-spaced, without quotation marks. Alexander Pope once wrote,

> 'Tis with our judgments as our watches; none
> Go just alike, yet each believes his own.
> In poets as true genius is but rare,
> True taste as seldom is the critic's share.

You should always remember that you must footnote when you use the words or ideas of another. If you don't, you will be guilty of plagiarism — offering another person's work as your own.

It is worth emphasizing that not only direct quotations demand footnoting. If you paraphrase from a source, you must use a footnote; if you borrow an important concept or term from a source, you must use a footnote. Any material in your papers which is not original, or is not common knowledge, requires a footnote.

Some of the ways writers incorporate quotations or information from another source into their writing are shown in the examples below. You will recall that it is standard American practice to place any necessary additional comma or period, when used at the end of a clause or sentence, inside the quotation marks. Note that quotation marks are omitted for the indirect quotation.

In each of the following quotations or paraphrases the writer has mentioned the source from which he is borrowing. Such attribution in the text of your own paper does not replace footnotes, although it does help the reader follow your writing smoothly.

1. According to Frederick Lewis Allen, author of *The Lords of Creation*, the men who were investing in stock in 1929 were mostly "well groomed, conservatively and impeccably tailored, pleasant-voiced, easy and courteous in address."[1]

2. Frederick Lewis Allen describes those men shortly before the stock crash. "The men whom we see about us as we stand in the Wall Street of 1929 and survey the passing crowd are mostly well groomed, conservatively and impeccably tailored, pleasant-voiced, easy and courteous in address."[2]

3. In *Culture and Anarchy* Matthew Arnold maintains that culture has its origin "in the love of perfection" rather than in curiosity. He goes on to say:

    And because men are all members of one great whole, and the sympathy which is in human nature will not allow one member to be indifferent to the rest or to have a perfect welfare independent of the rest, the expansion of our humanity, to suit the idea of perfection which culture forms, must be a *general* expansion. Perfection, as culture conceives it, is not possible while the individual remains isolated.[3]

4. Fowler, in his *Dictionary of Modern English Usage*, defines irony as "a form of utterance that postulates a double audience."[4]

5. It is Richard Hofstadter who said that the New Deal, for all its agreements to reduce tariffs, was essentially isolationist.[5] (This is an indirect quotation.)

6. And we must not forget "the heart's reasons": love and emotion have their logic too, as Pascal has reminded us.[6]

Footnotes and Bibliography

Footnotes

A footnote must be useful, not ornamental. It identifies the source of your quotation, paraphrase, or reference so that your reader can find the original easily should he wish to pursue it. It permits you to acknowledge with clarity and courtesy other people's ideas and words that you have used.

For the sake of clarity, footnotes are brief (using abbreviations whenever possible) and are written in a uniform way. The following sequence of information is the conventional form:

> The author's name in normal order (John Q. Smith; not Smith, John Q.)
>
> The title of the book, underlined to signify italics.
>
> The city of publication, the name of the publisher, the date of publication — all within one set of parentheses.
>
> The page number referred to.

When you have quoted or paraphrased, you send your reader to the footnote by placing the footnote number immediately after the quotation, and raised on the line, like this.[1] The notes should be numbered consecutively.   Literally, footnotes appear at the foot of each page; but for convenience you may choose to place your notes at the end of the paper, where they become literally "endnotes." Endnotes must be numbered consecutively throughout, of course, to avoid confusion. For our purposes in the following discussion, the word "footnotes" means either footnotes or endnotes.

Footnotes for Books

1. Book, one author

[1]Jessica Mitford, *The American Way of Death* (New York: Simon and Schuster, 1963), p. 245.

2. Book, more than one author

[2]C. Hugh Holman, William Flint Thrall, and Addison Hibbard, *A Handbook to Literature*, 3rd ed. (Indianapolis: Bobbs-Merrill, 1972), pp. 108-09.

3. Essay in a Book Edited by another person

[3]Geoffrey Tillotson, "Authorial Presence: Some Observations," in *Imagined Worlds: Essays on Some English Novels and Novelists in Honour of John Butt*, ed. Maynard Mack and Ian Gregor (London: Methuen, 1968), pp. 215-23.

4. Play or Poem in an Anthology

[4]Joe Orton, "What the Butler Saw," in *Joe Orton: The Complete Plays* (New York: Grove Press, 1977), p. 368.

If the original publication date of the play is important to your thesis, it is proper to add the information in the parentheses: (New York: Grove Press, 1977, orig. pub. London: Methuen, 1969, rev. 1976), p. 368.

5. Reference Work

There are more conflicting instructions in different handbooks about how to annotate encyclopaedia references than about any other kind of footnote. Simply be accurate and helpful to your reader. For major reference works like *Encyclopaedia Britannica* there is little confusion about the publisher, which can be omitted; but there are crucial distinctions about which edition you have consulted. We offer two acceptable models for each kind of entry — the signed and the unsigned articles.

a. Signed Articles

[5] Cyrus Henry Hoy, "Comedy," in *Encyclopedia Britannica: Macropaedia*, 15th ed., 1974, vol. 4, pp. 958-967.

> or

[5] *Encyclopaedia Britannica: Macropaedia*, 15th ed., 1974, "Comedy," by Cyrus Henry Hoy.

The first form is traditional, but the abbreviated information in the second form is really all that the reader requires if he wishes to consult your source. Since entries in encyclopaedias are alphabetical, even the page numbers are unnecessary in your footnote.

b. Unsigned Articles

[5] "Comedy," *Encyclopaedia Britannica*, 11th ed., 1910, vol. 6, p. 759.

> or

[5] *Encyclopaedia Britannica*, 11th ed., 1910, "Comedy."

6. Anonymous Book

[6]*Paperbound Books in Print: Spring 1974* (New York: Bowker, 1974), p. 1211.

7. Modern Reprint of an Old Edition

[7]John Stow, *A Survey of London:* Reprinted from the Text of 1603, ed. Charles Lethbridge Kingsford, 2 vols. (Oxford: Clarendon Press, 1971 corrected reprint of 1908 ed.), p. 41.

8. Translation

[8]Paul Hazard, *The European Mind, 1680-1715*, trans. J. Lewis May (Harmondsworth: Penguin, 1964 rep. of 1953 ed. Orig. French ed., 1935), p. 277.

Because of a complicated publishing history — the book is a paperback reprint (1964) of a London translation (1953) of a French book (1935) — this footnote appears painfully cluttered. You must use your judgment about whether it is important to include the 1953 or 1935 information for your reader.

9. Second References

Second (and later) references to these same sources should be significantly condensed, avoiding the obscure Latin abbreviations *(ibid., op. cit.)* that are more pedantic than clear.

[9]Mitford, p. 249.

10. Newspaper Article

[10]Joseph Cooper, "Press vs. Police," *New York Times*, 31 July 1980, p. A19.

After the date you may choose to include the name of the edition of the newspaper ("City Edition," in this case) and the column numbers ("cols. 1-2") because different editions sometimes change the locations of articles. There is no need to list the Volume and Number for newspapers — the date will suffice.

11. Magazine Article

[11]William Davenport, "Bordeaux — Fine Wines and Fiery Gascons," *National Geographic*, 158 (August 1980), pp. 233-259.

The "158" signifies the volume number. Different manuals offer different forms for this kind of note — some omitting the volume number if you have the date, others omitting the month if you have the volume number and if the pages are numbered consecutively through the entire volume. The only point to keep in mind is not the liturgy of footnoting, but the common sense of making certain that your reader can easily locate your source. Then be consistent in your form throughout your own paper.

Miscellaneous Footnotes

12. Unpublished Source

[12]Hilary Nash, "Cognac — The Region and its Product," unpublished essay written for English Competence course at Phillips Academy, 20 February 1980, p. 3.

13. Interviews and Conversations

[13]Interview with Hilary Nash, 5 March 1980, at Andover, Massachusetts.

Do not be embarrassed to acknowledge obtaining information informally, even from classmates. To omit that proper documentation is plagiarism.

If the work referred to is identified thoroughly, including the specific edition, in the context of the paragraph or in the heading of a book review, the writer may eliminate footnotes by simply giving page references in parentheses.

Bibliography

A bibliography is a list at the end of a work of all the books and articles the writer has consulted in whole or in part to write his paper, even if he has used no specific information from these works. It does *not* include works he has not actually consulted. The entries are in alphabetical order according to each author's last name. If no author is given, the entry begins with the title (or headline) of the piece. Each entry resembles the footnote, except that

> no number precedes the entry;
>
> the author's name is written last name first (to facilitate alphabetical order);

periods separate each item instead of commas; no parentheses are used; retain colon and comma in the publishing information;

page numbers are given only for articles included in a larger publication;

the bibliographical entry begins at the left margin, and all further lines for that entry are indented. This convention is designed for the reader's ease when he skims the entries looking for a title.

Bibliographical Entries for Books

1. **Book, One Author**

   Mitford, Jessica. *The American Way of Death.* New York: Simon and Schuster, 1963.

2. **Book, more than One Author**

   Holman, C. Hugh, William Flint Thrall, and Addison Hibbard. *A Handbook to Literature.* 3rd ed. Indianapolis: Bobbs-Merrill, 1972.

   Only the first author's name is listed in reversed order, for alphabetizing.

3. **Essay in a Book edited by another person**

   Tillotson, Geoffrey. "Authorial Presence: Some Observations." In *Imagined Worlds: Essays on Some English Novels and Novelists in Honour of John Butt.* Ed. Maynard Mack and Ian Gregor. London: Methuen, 1968.

4. **Play or Poem in an Anthology**

   Orton, Joe. "What the Butler Saw." In *Joe Orton: The Complete Plays.* New York: Grove Press, 1977. Orig. pub. London, 1969, rev. 1976.

5a. **Reference Work, Signed Article**

   Hoy, Cyrus Henry. "Comedy." *Encyclopaedia Britannica: Macropaedia.* 15th ed. 1974.

5b. **Reference Work, Unsigned Article**

   "Comedy." *Encyclopaedia Britannica.* 11th ed. 1910.

6. **Anonymous Book**

   Paperbound Books in Print: Spring 1974. New York: Bowker, 1974.

7. **Modern Reprint of an Old Edition**

   Stow, John. *A Survey of London:* Reprinted from the Text of 1603. Ed. Charles Lethbridge Kingsford. 2 vols. Oxford: Clarendon Press, 1971 corrected reprint of 1908 ed.

8. **Translation**

   Hazard, Paul. *The European Mind, 1680-1715.* Trans. J. Lewis May. Harmondsworth: Penguin, 1964 rep. of 1953 ed. Orig. French ed., 1935.

In the bibliography you must give complete information about translation and reprint. In the footnote you are invited to use your judgment about how much of that information is necessary.

Bibliographical Entries for Periodicals

9. Newspaper Article

Cooper, Joseph. "Press vs. Police." *New York Times*, City Ed. 31 July 1980, p. A19, cols. 1-2.

10. Magazine Article

Davenport, William. "Bordeaux — Fine Wines and Fiery Gascons." *National Geographic*, 158 (August 1980), pp. 233-259.

Miscellaneous Bibliographical Entries

11. Unpublished Source

Nash, Hilary. "Cognac — The Region and its Product." Unpublished essay written for English Competence course at Phillips Academy, 20 February 1980.

12. Interviews and Conversations

Nash, Hilary. Personal Interview. 5 March 1980.

The Business Letter

The business letter consists of six parts:

1. The Heading

2. The Inside Address

3. The Salutation

4. The Body

5. The Complimentary Close

6. The Signature

Besides letters of application (for a job, for admission to college), you may be writing letters of inquiry, condolence, gratitude, and complaint. Not all of these will demand the formality of the business letter. However, when writing to a firm or to someone who doesn't know you, you should remember that your letter will serve as an introduction. Spelling errors, awkward phraseology, inane questions — these will hardly present you in a flattering light. Carefully center your letter on the page.

Box 72
1. Phillips Academy
Andover, MA 01810
April 9, 1981

(6 spaces)
Mr. John Dalton, Camp Director
2. Camp Deerfoot
Deerfoot, PA 19194
(2 spaces)
3. Dear Mr. Dalton:
(2 spaces)
 Last summer I served as counselor at Camp Winnegoosie in Auburn, Maine. The summer before, I worked at Camp Greylock in western Massachusetts. This summer I would like to work in your camp and am writing in response to the advertisement in the Sunday *New York Times.*

 My special interests are ornithology, rock climbing, and creative
4. writing. Lest I sound too much of a "loner," I should also mention that this past year I was captain of the varsity basketball team.

 Should you wish recommendations, please write to the following:

 Mr. Raymond Foy, Camp Director
 Camp Winnegoosie
 Auburn, **ME** 04210

 Mr. Guy Howser, Basketball Coach
 Phillips Academy
 Andover, **MA** 01810

 I look forward to hearing from you.
(2 spaces)
        5. Sincerely,

(4 spaces)   *(Signature)*

        6. Anthony King
          (only if letter is typed)

VI.
Skills for Reading and Writing

V. Andover, Massachusetts, 1979   **Arno Rafael Minkkinen**

Reading Comprehension for Nonfiction

To read a specific work effectively, you may find some specific reading methods helpful.

Previewing

Skimming

Scanning

Note-Taking

Summarizing

Selecting Core Ideas

Examining Consequences

Listing Questions

Comparing (to other relevant passages)

The preview is a rapid assessment of the form and content of a passage. Merely turn through the pages of the passage you are about to read and look for headings, sub-headings, words that are italicized or capitalized. Read the opening and closing paragraphs. The preview acquaints you with what is to follow. Before you actually read the passage you may wish to skim or scan it. Skimming is forcing yourself to read very quickly through a passage, seeking a broad view of the subject. Scanning is hunting for a certain detail or fact, ignoring any other information as you move rapidly from page to page. Sometimes after reading a passage, you may wish to scan simply to review a detail that should be considered in your summary.

With the general objectives listed above in mind, you are ready to begin. Take a preview, then skim. If there is a word or heading that you need to check, scan back through the passage. You are prepared to read now. Be on the alert for the thesis statement, major topics, and important details. Take notes, if necessary. After you have finished reading, you might skim over the passage once more before you make the summary. In most cases, the summary will be a mental one; it will include the thesis statement and the major topics. Next select the core ideas, ones that you judge will be important to remember. Finally, make a tentative evaluation by considering the consequences of the thesis and any questions the passage might raise. Recall that evaluation is truly the domain of the scholar and the critic. However, you would be remiss if you didn't ask yourself certain obvious questions. Is the writer fair, or biased? Is his thesis tenable? Does it relate to anything you have read or heard before?

Reading Carefully and Sensibly

If you are to comprehend with accuracy a passage you wish to read, you should first rid yourself of preconceptions about the content or purpose of that passage. The subject may be population control or transcendental meditation. You may feel strongly that every family should be limited to two children. Or you may dismiss meditation as a hoax. In either case, these attitudes can inhibit an intelligent reading of the passage. Because of them, you may stubbornly resist new information on the subject or the writer's argument.

To read well, you must allow the writer to speak in his own voice, to have his style as you have yours. Like a judge, then, you must possess an open mind. You must weigh all of the facts before offering your opinion or making an evaluation. Particularly when reading nonfiction, you must not prejudge the writer. You may dislike his political stance. You may find his views on capital punishment too liberal. Nevertheless, to judge his writing fairly, you must suspend your personal bias.

Suppose that the following statement were made by a convict who had served a prison sentence for embezzlement. What are the preconceptions that you must guard against in reading this statement? What problems are involved in evaluating the accuracy of this statement?

> Life in the state pen isn't so bad. I had my own cell and some privacy, though at times the guards harassed me. I got a lot of reading done. Read some good books — as much of Faulkner, Steinbeck, Gide, and Genet as I could get my hands on. You can steer clear of trouble while you're in there; or you can get in deeper than ever you were on the outside. I know several guys who were stashing away piles of dough. One was printing up his own money in a nearby town and the other was head of a drug ring that reached clear out to Seattle. It's fairly easy to operate from behind bars. Some of the guards are soft touches; and occasionally new guys and visitors bring stuff in.

Once you have rid yourself of preconceptions, you should read alertly, and without absolute faith in the reliability of the writer. Remember the writer may choose to hide behind a mask or persona. A satirist like Jonathan Swift or Art Buchwald may use a persona to applaud the very position he deplores, counting on the reader to detect the folly of that position.

Paraphrase and Summary

A skillful reader has such an understanding of what he has read that he may, if necessary, paraphrase it, write a sentence summary of it, abridge it into a short paragraph summary, or even condense it to a careful topic or paragraph outline. Indeed, when he is reading difficult prose or poetry, the skillful reader probably does one or more of these procedures subconsciously. The best way to develop these skills, of course, is consciously, on paper.

Paraphrase

A paraphrase is a restatement of the original into your own idiomatic prose for ease of understanding, preserving the original person and tone. It is usually as long as the original, sometimes for poetry slightly longer. (To write something considerably longer than the original by including analysis of nuances is to move from paraphrase to explication.)

The following paragraph is from John Henry Newman's *The Idea of a University*.

> This then is how I should solve the fallacy, for so I must call it, by which Locke and his disciples would frighten us from cultivating the intellect, under the notion that no education is useful which does not teach us some temporal calling, or some mechanical art, or some physical secret. I say that a cultivated intellect, because it is a good in itself, brings with it a power and a grace to every work and occupation which it undertakes, and enables us to be more useful, and to a greater number. There is a duty we owe to human society as such, to the state to which we belong, to the sphere in which we move, to the individuals towards whom we are variously related, and whom we successively encounter in life; and that philosophical or liberal education, as I have called it, which is the proper function of a University, if it refuses the foremost place to professional interests, does but postpone them to the formation of the citizen, and, while it subserves the larger interests or philanthropy, prepares also for the successful prosecution of those merely personal objects, which at first sight it seems to disparage.

Here is a paraphrase of it:

> This is how I correct the error in logic, for I believe it is an error, which Locke and his followers use to steer us away from developing our ability to think intelligently and our capacity for knowledge. They claim that the only useful education is that which teaches us an occupation, a process, or a scientific fact. I say that a man

equipped with wide knowledge and the ability to think sharply will be well-suited for any occupation, and he will do greater good for more people because of his wide-ranging education. We each have a responsibility to mankind, to our country, to our community, to our friends and acquaintances. We will be better able to fulfill this responsibility if we receive the broad, thought-provoking education which a university ought to provide, instead of mere professional training. Education for occupation should, during the university years, come only after development of cultural and social awareness. Furthermore this awareness, instead of hindering attainment of personal goals, aids us in attaining them.

Paraphrasing requires understanding every word of the original passage. Consult the dictionary for any words you do not know. It would be foolish to attempt a paraphrase of Newman's paragraph if you were unclear on the meanings of words like *cultivating, temporal, liberal,* and *philanthrophy.* In a paraphrase, you may retain simple words and constructions from the original.

Summary

Whereas a paraphrase is about the same length as the original, a summary is an abridgement of a work, using one's own words but preserving the author's form and tone (especially the emphasis and subordination). It includes all the important ideas from the original. *It does not add new ideas or introduce even the slightest bias that is not found in the original.*

Sentence Summary.   The sentence summary is a one-sentence abridgement. It might paraphrase the topic sentence of the paragraph, though it usually includes more than the topic sentence does; it attempts to assert all of the ideas in the paragraph, not merely the main idea. Below is a paragraph from *The Encyclopaedia Britannica,* Eleventh Edition, on the development of Greek literature.

> The steps by which Attic prose style was developed, and the principal forms which it assumed, can be traced most clearly in the Attic orators. Every Athenian citizen who aspired to take part in the affairs of the city, or even to be qualified for self-defense, before a law-court, was required to have some degree of skill in public speaking; and an Athenian audience looked upon public debate, whether political or forensic, as a competitive trial of proficiency in a fine

art. Hence the speaker, no less than the writer, was necessarily a student of finished expression; and oratory had a more direct influence on the general structure of literary prose than has ever perhaps been the case elsewhere. A systematic rhetoric took its rise in Sicily, where Corax of Syracuse (466 B.C.) devised his *Art of Words* to assist those who were pleading before the law-courts; and it was brought to Athens by his disciple Tisias. The teaching of the Sophists, again, directed attention, though in a superficial and imperfect way, to the elements of grammar and logic; and Georgias of Leontini — whose declamation, however turgid, must have been striking — gave an impulse at Athens to the taste for elaborate rhetorical brilliancy.

Here is a sentence summary of the paragraph:

Athenian prose style was strongly influenced by oratory, since ability in rhetoric was both a practical necessity for many citizens and an art admired by all.

Paragraph Summary.   The paragraph summary is an abridgement requiring more than one sentence. Its ratio to the size of the original will vary widely from work to work; but one-quarter to one-third the length of the original is a reasonable average — obviously longer with a detailed and complex paragraph. In all other respects the same criteria hold for the paragraph summary as for the sentence summary: *use your own words, preserve the original form and tone, add nothing.*

A selection from Theodore Dreiser's novel *Sister Carrie:*

Here was a type of the travelling canvasser for a manufacturing house — a class which at that time was first being dubbed by the slang of the day "drummers." He came within the meaning of a still newer term, which had sprung into general use among Americans in 1880, and which concisely expressed the thought of one whose dress or manners are calculated to elicit the admiration of susceptible young women — a "masher." His suit was of a striped and crossed pattern of brown wool, new at that time, but since become familiar as a business suit. The low crotch of the vest revealed a stiff shirt bosom of white and pink stripes. From coat sleeves protruded a pair of linen cuffs of the same pattern, fastened with large, gold plate buttons set with the common yellow agates known as "cat's-eyes." His fingers bore several rings — one, the ever-enduring heavy seal — and from his vest dangled a neat gold watch chain, from which was suspended the secret insignia of the Order of Elks. The whole suit was rather tight-fitting, and was finished off with heavy-soled tan shoes, highly polished, and the grey fedora hat. He was, for the order of intellect represented, attractive, and whatever he had to recommend him you may be sure was not lost upon Carrie, in this, her first glance.

Lest this order of individual should permanently pass, let me put down some of the most striking characteristics of his most successful manner and method. Good clothes, of course, were the first essential, the things without which he was nothing. A strong physical nature, actuated by a keen desire for the feminine, was the next. A mind free of any consideration of the problems or forces of the world and actuated not by greed, but an insatiable love of variable pleasure. His method was always simple. Its principal element was daring, backed, of course, by an intense desire and admiration for the sex. Let him meet with a young woman once and he would approach her with an air of kindly familiarity, not unmixed with pleading, which would result in most cases in a tolerant acceptance. If she showed any tendency to coquetry he would be apt to straighten her tie, or if she "took up" with him at all, to call her by her first name. If he visited a department store it was to lounge familiarly over the counter and ask some leading questions. In more exclusive circles, on the train or in waiting stations, he went slower. If some seemingly vulnerable object appeared he was all attention — to pass the compliments of the day, to lead the way to the parlor car, carrying her grip, or, failing that, to take a seat next to her with the hope of being able to court her to her destination. Pillows, books, a footstool, the shade lowered; all these figured in the things which he could do. If, when she reached her destination he did not alight and attend her baggage for her, it was because, in his own estimation, he had signally failed.

A woman should some day write the complete philosophy of clothes. No matter how young, it is one of the things she wholly comprehends. There is an indescribably faint line in the matter of man's apparel which somehow divides for her those who are worth glancing at and those who are not. Once an individual has passed this faint line on the way downward he will get no glance from her. There is another line at which the dress of a man will cause her to study her own. This line the individual at her elbow now marked for Carrie. She became conscious of an inequality. Her own plain blue dress, with its black cotton tape trimmings, now seemed to her shabby. She felt the worn state of her shoes.

Below is a paragraph summary of the excerpt from *Sister Carrie:*

> This travelling salesman of the late 1800s known as a "masher" took great care with his clothes, which were colorful, ornate, fashionable. Let me speak of his quaintness; his clothes were designed to be attractive to women, and Carrie found them so. There was something unique about his manner as well, especially in his approach to women. He was bold and familiar upon the slightest acquaintance. A woman understands the significance of a man's clothes; from them she can tell if a man is worthy of her attention, and at times she finds herself using them to judge her own apparel, as Carrie was now doing, unfavorably to herself.

Note that this paragraph summary lacks coherence: there is a clear break in idea between the fourth and fifth sentences. When you are writing a paragraph summary of a complex or wide-ranging passage, you may well have trouble achieving unity and coherence in your own paragraph. What is important, however, is preserving the sense and emphasis of the original. You may wish to write your sentences in a list instead of in a paragraph.

It is not necessary to devote a sentence to each paragraph of the original. The ideas in some paragraphs may be included in phrases or subordinate clauses, while those in more important paragraphs may well deserve two sentences in your summary.

Exercises

A. Write a summary sentence for the following two paragraphs. Then write a summary paragraph of the selection. Are you able to include all the major ideas?

England is full of manly, clever, well-bred men who possess the talent of writing off-hand pungent paragraphs, expressing with clearness and courage their opinion on any person or performance. Valuable or not, it is a skill that is rarely found, out of the English journals. The English do this, as they write poetry, as they ride and box, by being educated to it. Hundreds of clever Praeds and Frerers and Froudes and Hoods and Hooks and Maginns and Mills and Macaulays, make poems, or short essays for a journal, as they make speeches in Parliament and on the hustings, or as they shoot and ride. It is a quite accidental and arbitrary direction of their general ability. Rude health and spirits, an Oxford education and the habits of society are implied, but not a ray of genius. It comes of the crowded state of the professions, the violent interest which all men take in politics, the facility of experimenting in the journals, and high pay.

The most conspicuous result of this talent is the Times newspaper. No power in England is more felt, more feared, or more obeyed. What you read in the morning in that journal, you shall hear in the evening in all society. It has ears everywhere, and its information is earliest, completest and surest. It has risen, year by year, and victory by victory, to its present authority. I asked one of its old contributors whether it had once been abler than it is now? "Never," he said; "these are its palmiest days." It has shown those qualities which are dear to Englishmen, unflinching adherence to its objects, prodigal intellectual ability and a towering assurance, backed by the perfect organization in its printing-house and its world-wide network of correspondence and reports. It has its own history and famous trophies. In 1820, it adopted the cause of Queen Caroline, and carried it against the king. It adopted a poor-law system, and almost alone lifted it through. When Lord Brougham was in power, it decided against him, and pulled him down. It declared war against Ireland, and conquered it. It adopted the League against the Corn Laws, and, when Cobden had begun to despair, it announced his triumph. It denounced and discredited the French Republic of 1848, and checked every sympathy with it in England, until it had enrolled 200,000 special constables to watch the Chartists and make them ridiculous on the 10th April. It first denounced and then adopted the new French Empire, and urged the French Alliance and its results. It has entered into each municipal, literary and social question,

almost with a controlling voice. It has done bold and seasonable service in exposing frauds which threatened the commercial community. Meantime, it attacks its rivals by perfecting its printing machinery, and will drive them out of circulation; for the only limit to the circulation of The Times is the impossibility of printing copies fast enough; since a daily paper can only be new and seasonable for a few hours. It will kill all but that paper which is diametrically in opposition; since many papers, first and last, have lived by their attacks on the leading journal. (Ralph Waldo Emerson, "The Times" from *English Traits)*

B. What method of development is used in this excerpt from Hamilton Wright Mabie's essay "Theocritus on Cape Cod"? Write a paragraph summary of the passage.

Cape Cod lies at the other end of the world from Sicily not only in distance, but in the look of it, the lay of it, the way of it. It is so far off that it offers a base from which one may get a fresh view of Theocritus.

There are very pleasant villages on the Cape, in the wide shade of ancient elms, set deep in the old-time New England quiet. For there was a time before the arrival of the Syrians, the Armenians, and the automobile, when New England was in a meditative mood. But Cape Cod is really a ridge of sand with a backbone of soil, rashly thrust into the Atlantic, and as fluent and volatile, so to speak, as one of those far Western rivers that are shifting currents sublimely indifferent to private ownership. The Cape does not lack stability, but it shifts its lines with easy disregard of charts and boundaries, and remains stable only at its center; it is always fraying at the edges. It lies, too, on the western edge of the ocean stream, where the forces of land and sea are often at war and the palette of colors is limited. The sirocco does not sift fine sand through every crevice and fill the heart of man with murderous impulses: but the east wind diffuses a kind of elemental depression.

Sicily, on the other hand, is high-built on rocky foundations, and is the wide-spreading reach of a great volcano sloping broadly and leisurely to the sea. It is often shaken at its center, but the sea does not take from nor add to its substance at will. It lies in the very heart of a sea of such ravishing color that by sheer fecundity of beauty it has given birth to a vast fellowship of gods and divinely fashioned creatures; its slopes are white with billowy masses of almond blossoms in that earlier spring which is late winter on Cape Cod; while gray-green, gnarled, and twisted olive trees bear witness 151 to the passionate moods of the Mediterranean, mother of poetry, comedy, and tragedy, often asleep in a dream of beauty in which the shadowy figures of the oldest time move, often as violent as the North Atlantic when March torments it with furious moods. For the Mediterranean is as seductive, beguiling, and uncertain of temper as Cleopatra, as radiant as Hera, as voluptuous as Aphrodite. Put in terms of color, it is as different from the sea round Cape Cod as a picture by Sorolla is different from a picture by Mauve.

The Logic of Nonfiction Prose

In reading nonfiction of any sort (news reports, editorials, historical articles, political statements, literary criticisms, and — above all — advertisements) you must constantly test the logic of the writing. In your own writing you must employ logic as well.

Logic is the reasoning process used to arrive at an accurate conclusion or judgment. If something is illogical, its reasoning is inaccurate in one or more ways.

Each piece of effective writing has a proof, even if the work is not an exposition or an argument. Whether a writer selects a certain method of development or merely writes a topic sentence, his prose is governed by logic.

The body of your paragraph, letter, or composition will work out the proof of the topic sentence or thesis statement. A coherent structure is crucial to logical development of your argument. Two common methods used to organize this sort of writing are inductive structure and deductive structure.

Inductive structure proceeds from the observation of specific examples to a general conclusion. If you use an inductive structure, be sure to have a number of examples adequate to prove your point. Because that point is stated at the end of the piece of writing, it should be emphatic and convincing.

Whereas inductive structure proceeds from specific details to a generalization, deductive structure begins with a generalization and works out its proof with specific details. If you use a deductive structure, state your point clearly at the beginning.

The first of these two paragraphs about botulism food poisoning, paraphrased from *Botany*, by C.L. Wilson and W.E. Loomis, uses inductive structure; the second uses deductive structure.

> The bacillus which causes botulism food poisoning belongs to the same genus as that which causes tetanus. Botulism results from consumption of food containing a preformed exotoxin, the most potent toxin known to man. One ounce of this toxin would be enough to kill 400 million people; the mortality rate for those who contract botulism approaches 70 per cent. Most cases of botulism come from eating home-canned foods. Home canning by boiling alone cannot kill the botulism spores in low-acid foods. Although incidences of botulism poisoning in commercially-prepared foods is almost non-existent, botulism is a deadly threat to man.

Botulism food poisoning represents a serious danger to man. The bacillus which causes it, of the same genus as that which causes tetanus, is the most potent known. One ounce of the preformed exotoxin which causes the disease could kill 400 million people; the mortality rate for those who contract botulism poisoning approaches 70 per cent. Home-canned foods are the chief source of botulism, since canning by boiling alone cannot kill the botulism spores in low-acid foods. Fortunately, incidence of botulism in commercially prepared foods is almost unknown.

Violations of Logical Development

When you read a piece of nonfiction, you should be constantly alert for fallacies — violations of logic which may render the writing unclear or invalid. The presence of fallacies may indicate that a writer is trying to mislead his readers, or simply that he is too lazy or too careless to do a good job presenting and developing his material. Some of the more common fallacies are listed below.

A. **Non Sequitur** (Latin for "it does not follow")

   If a writer draws a conclusion unjustified by, or unrelated to, the facts or ideas which precede it, he has created a *non sequitur*.

   > Since girls were admitted to this college, academic achievement has gone up. Girls are, therefore, more industrious and more intelligent than boys.

B. **Hasty Generalization**

   If a writer bases a conclusion on evidence that is clearly insufficient, he has committed the fallacy called hasty generalization. While there exists no rule to determine how many examples are enough to prove a given point, in many cases the violation of logic is obvious.

   > I hate football. You and Sheila hate football. Doesn't everyone hate football?

   > Both the Soviet Union and East Germany have recently introduced possibilities for individual free enterprise. Thus we see that the Communist countries are beginning to turn to capitalism to build up their economies.

C. **False Premise**

   If the premise upon which an argument is based is false, the argument has no logical validity. Be alert for false premises in such reasoning as this:

   > All ocean creatures are cold-blooded. The blue whale lives in the ocean, and therefore is cold-blooded.

D. Emotionalism

Writing that unjustifiably appeals to the emotions while pretending to appeal to the intellect is another violation of logic. In order to evaluate the writer's position, the reader must separate the argument from connotative words and appeals to sentiment and sympathy.

> Sir/ The Supreme Court decision on capital punishment compels decent, hard-working citizens to provide free food, clothing, shelter, and recreation for social perverts who have murdered in cold blood. Of course, now that we have no capital punishment, our enlightened parole boards will eventually loose these creatures on society to begin the vicious cycle all over again. . . .

> Dear Sir:
>
> I write to you to suggest the name Rhoda Snodgrass as "Dallas Outstanding Teen-ager of the Month" for January. As her school counselor, I have seen the real suffering that Rhoda's family has been through since Mr. Snodgrass was laid off his job in August. The $1,000 scholarship that goes with the award will not only help Rhoda attend S.M.U. next year; it will also provide one bright spot for a family of five which has had much too much gloom in their lives. . . .

E. Poisoning the Well

Prejudicing a reader against an idea or person by using insinuation or unsupported value judgments is the logical equivalent of poisoning a well before one has a chance to drink from it.

> Of course, Billy has always been a liar, so I didn't believe what he told me, and I don't think you will believe it, either.

Just as a logical writer should not poison the well, neither should he sweeten it:

> Here is an excellent idea, and I want all of you to give it your closest attention.

F. Questionable Authority

Suppressing or distorting evidence to prove a point may be more than misuse of inductive structure; if it is done consciously, it is intellectual dishonesty. A more common danger is quoting out of context to give the quotation a slant that it really does not have. More common still (and more subtle) is making a subjective judgment in an authoritative tone that sounds objective. In the following quotation from *Time* by Robert Hughes, on what authority does the author make his assertions in the second sentence? Has he added any irrelevant details to slant the reader's opinion of the poet Rupert Brooke (poisoning the well)? Do you have any questions about the "one-to-twelve" ratio that the author mentions?

> One of the many tragedies of World War I was that it ruined a generation of artists and poets on both sides of the trenches. For every minor cult figure like Rupert Brooke, polishing his gung-ho stanzas and dying of a mosquito bite en route to the Dardenelles, a dozen real poets like Isaac Rosenberg and Wilfred Owen were cut down.

G. False Definition

A definition must establish a class to which a term belongs and differentiate that term from others in that class. It is important to remember that a true statement about a term is by no means necessarily a definition of it. We may write that a tomato is a garden plant that yields a pulpy red fruit. That statement is generally true; however, offered as a definition it is false. The fruit of the tomato plant is sometimes yellow, and countless tomatoes are grown in fields rather than in gardens. When you encounter a definition, you should examine it for accuracy. If the writer fails to have a clear understanding of the term or does not phrase it with precision, or both, he will probably create a false definition.

H. Begging the Question

If a writer assumes the truth of the idea he is attempting to prove and uses that assumption as part of his proof, he is arguing in a circle, or begging the question. His own thought is most likely foggy, and he confuses the reader as well.

> Throughout the history of Western society, woman's place has always been in the home. In recent years, spurred on by the rhetoric of women's lib, many women have rejected their

domestic duties to pursue careers. By and large, these "liberated" women have been unsuccessful, because in America women are properly equipped to handle only the role of housewife.

I. False Analogy

An analogy never *proves* a point; it is merely an illustration. An argument that is based upon the similarities between two unlike things is not logical. The fallacy is compounded when the writer exaggerates the similarities of two things which are not really comparable.

The American man of letters is strikingly similar to the extinct dodo bird. Like the dodo, his plumage is ornate, and unsuited to an environment of expedience and superficiality. As the dodo lays but a single egg, so the man of letters labors endlessly on his *magnum opus;* if it never hatches, he is content nonetheless. If he is driven out of one place, having exhausted the patience of his acquaintances, the man of letters will find another, more remote. As our modern society becomes less interested in supporting such an ungainly, unproductive creature, he is becoming increasingly rarer. Like his awkward aviary counterpart, the American man of letters will shortly lose his place in the world's ecological balance.

Exercises

A. Identify and be prepared to explain the fallacies in the following sentences.

1. Harry must be the one who broke the Coke machine in the club room. I saw him there last night.

2. Good poetry is always sad. That poem about wandering around like some cloud is too cheerful to mean much.

3. An end run will never work against this defense, but if you guys want to try it, I guess we can.

4. Fords last longer than Chevies. They are not much more expensive; they have many features; but the real reason you should choose a Ford is that it will give you a more durable car.

5. If we really want to help this great nation of ours survive this time of economic hardship, we should buy high quality American goods, made in the good old USA, instead of cheap foreign imports.

6. Dentists agree that Squeeze toothpaste is the best in preventing cavities and leaving your teeth sweet, clean, and hard.

7. I have been waiting a full hour here for a Frankford Ave. bus. They must not run on Fridays.

8. Paper clips are devices to hold papers together. They are a unique aid, which is very useful in any endeavor requiring paper processing, from businesses to schools.

9. Students ought to be able to use their notes for this examination. After all, doctors often consult their medical books for difficult diagnoses, don't they?

B. In a sentence or two for each, explain the problems in logical development of the two paragraphs below.

1. The chief cause of the slackening of output from the once prodigious pen of Paddy McEwen was simply indolence: in a word, the man was lazy. Three best sellers, and two lesser works — in sales, though many critics found them greater — then nothing, for four years. It is doubtful that he ever put pen to paper in all that time, though he lived in a fine style. In Paris, in Rome, in Acapulco, in Honolulu, Paddy (and his succession of women-friends) led a frenetic life. It is indeed a wonder that he did not expire from sheer activity of it all.

2. Benny Osterling is clearly the outstanding candidate for the presidency of our class. He is concerned about the school, eager to see it go in the right direction. Benny has a charming personality; he has been one of the most popular boys in the class since entering Morse High as a ninth grader. He has been instrumental in leading a number of important activities, including the fall Homecoming Dance and the Bake Sale, which made more than enough money for the new basketball scoreboard. Now, when the senior class needs a firm sense of direction toward the academic improvements of Morse High, Benny is head and shoulders above the other candidates.

VII.
Supplemental Material

X. Untitled   **Anthony Barboza**

Supplemental Material

The paragraphs in this section are chosen to illustrate some of the writing and reading skills that the preceding pages have discussed. For the most part, they illustrate good form. Many of these paragraphs can be studied for other virtues than the ones that are indicated above each section.

I. The Topic Sentence, Transitions, Coordination and Subordination

(1) Greek religion, as set forth in popular handbooks and even in more ambitious treatises, is an affair mainly of mythology, and moreover of mythology as seen through the medium of literature. In England, so far as I am aware, no serious attempt has been made to examine Greek ritual. Yet the facts of ritual are more easy definitely to ascertain, more permanent, and at least equally significant. What a people *does* in relation to its gods must always be one clue, and perhaps the safest, to what it *thinks*. The first preliminary to any scientific understanding of Greek religion is a minute examination of its ritual. (Jane Harrison, *Prolegomena to the Study of Greek Religion*)

(2) As a Shakespearean tragedy represents a conflict which terminates in a catastrophe, any such tragedy may roughly be divided into three parts. The first of these sets forth or expounds the situation, or state of affairs, out of which the conflict arises; and it may, therefore, be called the Exposition. The second deals with the definite beginning, the growth and the vicissitudes of the conflict. It forms accordingly the bulk of the play, comprising the Second, Third and Fourth Acts, and usually a part of the First and a part of the Fifth. The final section of the tragedy shows the issue of the conflict in a catastrophe. (A.C. Bradley, *Shakespearean Tragedy*)

(3) He was working in the steaming pit of hell; day after day, week after week — until now there was not an organ of his body that did its work without pain, until the sound of ocean breakers echoed in his head day and night, and the buildings swayed and danced before him as he went down the street. And from all the unending horror of this there was a respite, a deliverance — he could drink! He could forget the pain, he could slip off the burden; he would see clearly again, he would be master of his

brain, of his thoughts, of his will. His dead self would stir in him, and he would find himself laughing and cracking jokes with his companions — he would be a man again, and master of his life. (Upton Sinclair, *The Jungle*)

(4) Walpole was a short, dumpy man, weighing rather more than twenty stone. His arms and legs were short; his heavy head sprang almost straight from his shoulders. His features were large and coarse — square double chin, strongly marked black eyebrows, straight, thinnish mouth, with a thick, protruding underlip, a sharp emphatic nose. Yet about the face there were the undeniable marks of humour and intelligence which gave these strong features both animation and charm. The bright brown eyes and the mobile mouth whose corners seem almost to twitch in his more formal and wooden portraits rescued the face from the commonplace. The wide-spaced eyes gave him an air of surprised frankness, an openness that was curiously engaging and highly deceptive. As blunt and as outspoken as any man when he wished to be, yet he could be as supple and as subtle as a serpent. Above all he exuded power, an aspect of his character so obvious that many were disturbed by it, fearing and resenting his certainty, his desire for personal control. A character of such complexity, he had, throughout his life, been either loved or hated; sometimes both, but few, except perhaps his mother — a curiously opaque character — had been indifferent to him. Now in the noonday of his power he was the most sought-after man in the kingdom, the most feared, the most detested, and against him there was a snarling outcry of impotent rage. (J.H. Plumb, *The First Four Georges*)

(5) Survivors of the plague, finding themselves neither destroyed nor improved, could discover no Divine purpose in the pain they had suffered. God's purposes were usually mysterious, but this scourge had been too terrible to be accepted without questioning. If a disaster of such magnitude, the most lethal ever known, was a mere wanton act of God or perhaps not God's work at all, then the absolutes of a fixed order were loosed from their moorings. Minds that opened to admit these questions could never again be shut. Once people envisioned the possibility of change in a fixed order, the end of an age of submission came in sight; the turn to individual conscience lay ahead. To that extent the Black Death may have been the unrecognized beginning of modern man. (Barbara W. Tuchman, *A Distant Mirror*)

(6) As a result of his own puzzling, Einstein arrived at an unexpected but tremendously powerful formulation. He was able to demonstrate that neither time nor space has an objective, independent existence. Movements, speeds, distances could only be defined relative to one another. But once these perspectives are taken into account, it was, he believed, possible to derive the fundamental laws of nature. (Howard Gardner, *Psychology Today*, September 1980)

(7) Throughout decolonized Africa, rebel music and the social shock wave that accompanies it can be summed up in one volatile word: Fela. Fela Anikulapo-Kuti, a thirty-eight-year-old Nigerian singer and bandleader, has created a distinctly African music of political dissent. Fela (pronounced *FAY*-la) combines mesmeric African chants with the thunder of drums and electric instruments. He is the Third World's first real superstar. (Stephen Davis, *Saturday Review*, 22 July 1978)

(8) In the middle of all that frenzy out on the court, Oscar and I would usually butt heads in ways I'd remember. On many an afternoon, we'd eat a meal together, and then go out that night to kill each other. He knew that if he ran into me I was going to hit him, and he'd probably have been upset if I hadn't. And I knew that whenever I guarded him on a switch, Oscar would be dribbling with one hand and trying to club me to death with the other. This was what we called Oscar's "free foul," because the referees would never call it on him. (Bill Russell and Taylor Branch, *The New York Times Magazine*, 16 September 1979)

II. Unity, Coherence, Emphasis, Clarity, Concreteness

(9) The coffee-house must not be dismissed with a cursory mention. It might indeed at that time have been not improperly called a most important political institution. No Parliament had sat for years. The municipal council of the City had ceased to speak the sense of the citizens. Public meetings, harangues, resolutions, and the rest of modern machinery of agitation had not yet come into fashion. Nothing resembling the modern newspaper existed. In such circumstances the coffee-houses were

the chief organs through which the public opinion of the metropolis vented itself. (Lord Macaulay, *The History of England*)

(10) A cough and a tobacco stain on the second finger of her right hand told us that she was a heavy smoker, but we learned from the riding master's wife that Miss Gowrie steadily refused to take a cigarette anywhere near the Seminary and blinked with disapproval when she heard that other teachers did it. This watchfulness of conscience brooded likewise over her favorites; that is, her better students, for she knew no other measure. You could tell you were in Miss Gowrie's good graces by the bad-conduct marks she set firmly opposite your name in the school record book. In fact, in all her ways she was a stoic of the Roman mold, recalling that matron cited in Pliny, the terrible Arria, who, to encourage her husband to commit suicide, plunged a dagger into her own breast, drew it out, saying, "It doesn't hurt, Paetus," and handed it to him. (Mary McCarthy, *Memories of a Catholic Girlhood*)

(11) It looks as if Jacobi isn't home. The studio is dark, but from a doorway at the far end of the room, the 83-year-old photographer suddenly appears, her face emerging out of the darkness as if disembodied. Her wrinkles seem drawn on. Two dark eyes stare boldly out into the fog; they are mesmerizing. "Since you have an appointment you may come in," she says with a crisp German accent. She does not smile. She leads the way through the studio into the office adjoining it, and pulls up a chair for her visitor, close to the wood stove. She sits down at her desk. "Excuse me if I must continue to work." (Gaylen Moore, *The New York Times Magazine*, 16 September 1979)

(12) For such reasons it is that the memory of John Brown stands to-day as a mighty warning to his country. He saw, he felt in his soul the wrong and danger of that most daring and insolent system of human repression known as American slavery. He knew that in 1700 it would have cost something to overthrow slavery and establish liberty; and that by reason of cowardice and blindness the cost in 1800 was vastly larger but still not un-payable. He felt that by 1900 no human hand could pluck the vampire from the body of the land without doing the nation to death. He said in 1859, "Now is the accepted time." Now is the day to strike for a free nation. It will cost something — even

blood and suffering, but it will not cost as much as waiting. And he was right. Repression bred repression — serfdom bred slavery, until in 1861 the South was farther from freedom than in 1800. (W.E.B. DuBois, *John Brown)*

(13) More than one nation is finally remembered, long after its rulers have been buried and its armies dispersed, through its artists — the men and women who record in paint, stone, wood, cloth, clay, and music the struggle to extend the reach of the human spirit. An artist enriches not only his countrymen but every person on the planet. There is cause for celebration, therefore, in the news that the arts are penetrating more deeply than ever before into our national life. (John J. Veronis, *Saturday Review of the Arts,* April 1973)

(14) What was it in a Gelsey Kirkland or a Rudolph Nureyev that so charmed her? Not only grace and sleek beauty — something else. Spontaneity under control, an exquisite and soundless — she never heard the music — control of the body. She loved that surprise of ballet, that snap of airy poise when the body froze lithely in mid-air, then sprang back to earth. It always saddened her when finally a performance came to an end and the spell was shattered by applause and the harsh lights of reality.

(15) Knowledge of human nature is the beginning and end of political education, but several years of arduous study in the neighborhood of Westminster led Henry Adams to think that knowledge of English human nature had little or no value outside of England. In Paris, such a habit stood in one's way; in America, it roused all the instincts of native jealousy. The English mind was one-sided eccentric, systematically unsystematic, and logically illogical. The less one knew of it, the better. (Henry Adams, *The Education of Henry Adams)*

III. Methods of Paragraph Development, Person, Voice

(16) A second kind of courage is moral courage. The persons I have known, or have known of, who have great moral courage have

generally abhorred violence. Take, for example, Aleksander Solzhenitsyn, the Russian author who stood up alone against the might of the Soviet bureaucracy in protest against the inhuman and cruel treatment of men and women in Russian prison camps. His numerous books, written in the best prose of modern Russia, cry out against the crushing of any person, whether physically, psychologically, or spiritually. His moral courage stands out the more clearly since he is not a liberal, but a Russian nationalist. He became the symbol of a value lost sight of in a confused world — that the innate worth of a human being must be revered solely because of his or her humanity and regardless of his or her politics. A Dostoevskian character out of old Russia (as Stanley Kunitz describes him), Solzenitsyn proclaimed, "I would gladly give my life if it would advance the cause of truth." (Rollo May, *The Courage to Create*)

(17) The "horned hand" was a sign of recognition between the initiated. The index finger and the little finger were raised while the other fingers were turned down, recalling in a strange way certain heads of devils drawn in the Middle Ages. However, if occultists of more recent times are to be believed it is enough to hold up a "horned hand" to the light to make the devil helpless. In his play "Le Diable Amoureux" Cazotte brings on to the stage at one moment two men, both initiates, who recognise each other by making the sign of the "horned hand." (Maurice Bessy, *A Pictorial Essay of Magic and the Supernatural*)

(18) By the time James and Kate [Van DerZee] returned to New York in the spring of 1908, Harlem was, in James's words, "breaking loose." The process had already begun back in 1878-1881, before he ever arrived in New York, when Manhattan's three elevated railroad lines had been extended to 129th Street and plans had been made to push them even farther north. Harlem's major drawback as a residential area had always been its isolation from the core of the city. The northward extension of the elevated lines had made living in Harlem a more appealing prospect. Land speculators had moved in, purchasing land and erecting town houses and apartment buildings in anticipation of huge profits. In their frenzy of development, they inflated land prices, built too many buildings, and overextended themselves by investing too heavily in the promise, rather than the reality, of expanded transporta-

tion facilities. By 1904-1905, they realized what they had done. Rows of empty buildings faced the wide, tree-lined avenues — buildings that were producing no revenues but whose mortgage payments were still due at the bank every month. The elevated lines were nowhere near completion. Desperate to recoup their losses, speculators and realtors turned to the burgeoning Negro population downtown and found willing tenants in the occupants of the overcrowded, slum-ridden Tenderloin and San Juan Hill areas. To these blacks, Harlem was like the Promised Land, a "decent" neighborhood. Many of its new apartment houses had never been occupied, and if the rents were steep, well, blacks were used to being charged higher rents than whites anyway. They began to trickle into Harlem. (Jim Haskins, *James Van DerZee: The Picture-Takin' Man*)

(19) We feel uncomfortable standing here, some of us dressed up for the job parade, some of us in the sweat shirts and worn-down heels of the aimless unemployed. Cigarettes and matches protrude among us like little flags of tension; eyes shift away from even momentary meetings. We case each other on the sly, telling ourselves that we do not belong to this group, we have never had to stand in this line before, we do not really have to stand here now except that our friends have urged us to. (Adele Foy, *The New York Times*, 21 July 1980)

(20) Beyond the park, above steaming fields, a rainbow slipped into view; the fields ended in the notched dark border of a remote fir wood; part of the rainbow went across it, and that section of the forest edge shimmered most magically through the pale green and pink of the iridescent veil drawn before it: a tenderness and a glory that made poor relatives of the rhomboidal, colored reflections which the return of the sun had brought forth on the pavilion floor. (Vladimir Nabokov, *Speak, Memory*)

(21) Any general statement is like a cheque drawn on a bank. Its value depends on what is there to meet it. If Mr. Rockefeller draws a cheque for a million dollars it is good. If I draw one for a million it is a joke, a hoax, it has no value. If it is taken seriously, the writing of it becomes a criminal act. (Ezra Pound, *A B C of Reading*)

(22) How was it possible, I asked myself, to walk for an hour through the woods and see nothing worthy of note? I who cannot see find hundreds of things to interest me through mere touch. I feel the delicate symmetry of a leaf. I pass my hands lovingly about the smooth skin of a silver birch, or the rough, shaggy bark of a pine. In spring I touch the branches of trees hopefully in search of a bud, the first sign of awakening Nature after her winter's sleep. Occasionally, if I am very fortunate, I place my hand gently on a small tree and feel the happy quiver of a bird in full song. (Helen Keller, "Three Days to See")

(23) The first two weeks after her return represented to Mrs. Peniston the domestic equivalent of a religious retreat. She "went through" the linen and blankets in the precise spirit of the penitent exploring the inner folds of conscience; she sought for moths as the stricken soul seeks for lurking infirmities. The topmost shelf of every closet was made to yield up its secret, cellar and coal-bin were probed to their darkest depths and, as a final stage in the lustral rites, the entire house was swathed in penitential white and deluged with expiatory soap suds. (Edith Wharton, *The House of Mirth*)

(24) On another level, "Bellefleur" is fairy tale and myth, distraught literature. There is a walled garden, a decayed tower, a sinister cat, a swamp monster, a spider as big as a humming bird, a man who turns into a bear, a pond that breathes, a holy mountain (Mount Blanc), evil water (Lake Noir), a poet, a cannibal, a demon, a troll, a vampire, a hermaphrodite, a clairvoyant, an elf, silver foxes, white mist, hermits, sleepwalkers, religious maniacs, a halo and a missing pinkie finger, purple orchids more than a foot in diameter, "high-grade Arctic nitrogen-rich elk manure," bad copies of Italian Renaissance art, a monkey tree, a Russian olive, a cedar of Lebanon, mirrors, and jaws, a drum made of human skin and a clavichord occupied by a human soul. (John Leonard, *The New York Times*, 21 July 1980)

(25) There are basically two kinds of travel writers — those who fly around the world in airplanes and those who drive around the United States in cars. The international writer generally begins his article with a phrase like "Whenever I return to the rugged hills of the Basque country . . ." or "Sipping a dry jeriñac that made the roof of my mouth shout 'ole!" and will cloak the most desolate spot in the Sahara in a patina of savage romance. The

USA writer begins his ruminations with a simple declarative sentence like "I pulled into a gas station in Metairie and noticed the owner looked Cajun." The international stylist imitates Graham Greene, V.S. Pritchett, and *Gourmet* magazine. The national learns from Hemingway, Steinbeck, Kerouac, Hunter Thompson, and *Texas Monthly*. No matter where these writers go, their ensuing article is always favorable to the locale, the hotel rooms, and the food. There is always an out-of-the-way hole-in-the-wall where the bouillabaisse is sensational, but by the time the reader gets to town, the eatery's been closed down by the local board of health. (John Mariani, *Saturday Review*, 22 July 1978)

IV. Style, Figurative Language, Rhetorical, Patterns, Diction

(26) Well, I was perfectly honest and square with her; told her I hadn't a cent in the world but just the million-pound note she'd heard so much talk about, and *it* didn't belong to me, and that started her curiosity; and then I talked low, and told her the whole history right from the start, and it nearly killed her laughing. What in the nation she could find to laugh about *I* couldn't see, but there it was; every half-minute some new detail would fetch her, and I would have to stop as much as a minute and a half to give her a chance to settle down again. Why, she laughed herself lame — she did, indeed; I never saw anything like it. I mean I never saw a painful story — a story of a person's troubles and worries and fears — produce just *that* kind of effect before. So I loved her all the more, seeing she could be so cheerful when there wasn't anything to be cheerful about; for I might soon need that kind of wife, you know, the way things looked. (Mark Twain, "The £1,000,000 Bank Note")

(27) A man's life should be a stately march to a sweet but unheard music, and when to his fellows it shall seem irregular and in-harmonious, he will only be stepping to a livelier measure, or his nicer ear hurry him into a thousand symphonies and concor-dant variations. There will be no halt ever, but at most a marching on his post, or such a pause as is richer than any sound, when the melody runs into such depth and wildness as to be no longer heard, but implicitly consented to with the whole life and being. He will take a false step never, even in

Z. Untitled, 1977   **Starr Ockenzga**

the most arduous times, for then the music will not fail to swell into greater sweetness and volume, and itself rule the movement it inspired. (Henry David Thoreau, *The Journal of Henry David Thoreau*)

(28) During the whole of a dull, dark, and soundless day in the autumn of the year, when the clouds hung oppressively low in the heavens, I had been passing alone, on horseback, through a singularly dreary tract of country; and at length found myself, as the shades of the evening drew on, within view of the melancholy House of Usher. I know not how it was — but, with the first glimpse of the building, a sense of insufferable gloom pervaded my spirit. I say insufferable; for the feeling was unrelieved by any of that half-pleasurable because poetic sentiment, with which the mind usually receives even the sternest natural images of the desolate or terrible. I looked upon the scene before me — upon the mere house, and the simple landscape features of the domain, upon the bleak walls, upon the vacant eye-like windows, and upon a few rank sedges, and upon a few white trunks of decayed trees — with an utter depression of soul which I can compare to no earthly sensation more properly than to the after-dream of the reveller upon opium: the bitter lapse into everyday life, the hideous dropping off of the veil. (Edgar Allen Poe, "The Fall of the House of Usher")

(29) The military spirit is the most merciless, heartless and brutal in existence. It fosters an institution for which there is not even a pretense of justification. The soldier, to quote Tolstoi, is a professional man-killer. He does not kill for the love of it, like a savage, or in a passion, like a homicide. He is a cold-blooded, mechanical, obedient tool of his military superiors. He is ready to cut throats or scuttle a ship at the command of his ranking officer, without knowing or, perhaps, caring how, why or wherefore. I am supported in this contention by no less a military light than Gen. Funston. I quote from the latter's communication to the New York *Evening Post* of June 30, dealing with the case of Private William Buwalda, which caused such a stir all through the Northwest. "The first duty of an officer or enlisted man," says our noble warrior, "is unquestioning obedience and loyalty to the government to which he has sworn allegiance; it makes no difference whether he approves of that government or not." (Emma Goldman, "What I Believe")

(30) Thirty-five dead. Standing alone, the words were shocking enough. Still, it was only a number. Wicker tried for a moment to think of 35 bodies. Then 35 faces. He tried to think of 35 lives. But he had no idea who had lived or perished in the D-yard carnage, or how. He did not know if the youth in the cotton gloves was dead. He did not know if Brother Phillip Shields had come through alive, or Blair McDonald, or Michael and Art Smith, or Pappy Wald, or Champ, or Big Black, or any of the faceless men who had been out there beyond the arm-linked security chain or in the hostage circle. There was no way to tell whether any of the people he had known in D-yard were living or dead. There was only one flat and searing fact. Thirty-five dead. (Tom Wicker, *A Time to Die*)

(31) It turned out to be true. The face of the water, in time, became a wonderful book, a book that was dead language to the uneducated passenger, but which told its mind to me without reserve, delivering its most cherished secrets as clearly as if it uttered them with a voice. And it was not a book to be read once and thrown aside, for it had a new story to tell every day. Throughout the long twelve hundred miles there was never a page that was void of interest, never one that you could leave unread without loss, never one that you would want to skip, thinking you could find higher enjoyment in some other thing. There never was so wonderful a book written by man; never one whose interest was so absorbing, so unflagging, so sparklingly renewed with every reperusal. The passenger who could not read it was charmed with a peculiar sort of faint dimple on its surface (on the rare occasions when he did not overlook it altogether); but to the pilot that was an *italicized* passage; indeed, it was more than that, it was a legend of the largest capitals, with a string of shouting exclamation points at the end of it; for it meant that a wreck or a rock was buried there that could tear the life out of the strongest vessel that ever floated. It is the faintest and simplest expression the water ever makes, and the most hideous to a pilot's eye. In truth, the passenger who could not read this book saw nothing but all manner of pretty pictures in it, painted by the sun and shaded by the clouds, whereas to the trained eye these were not pictures at all, but the grimmest and most dead-earnest of reading matter. (Mark Twain, *Life on the Mississippi*)

(32) Of all the performing arts, dance had always held for her the most fascination. Listening to music seemed too passive, acting a bit too contrived (she hated following all the words). But dance had always thrilled her. She wished she had the agility and limberness to dance herself. She wished also she had the self-discipline to study dance. But alas, she was indolent by nature, addicted irrevocably to chocolate. Her body was short of limb, stout, heavy-boned.

(33) . . . No passion had ever touched him, for this was what passion meant: he had survived and maundered and pined, but where had been his deep ravage? The extraordinary thing we speak of was the sudden rush of the result of this question. The sight that had just met his eyes (a man mourning at the grave of his lover) named to him, as in letters of quick flame, something he had utterly, insanely missed, and what he had missed made these things a train of fire, made them mark themselves in an anguish of inward throbs. He had seen outside of his life, not learned it within, the way a woman was mourned when she had been loved for herself: such was the force of his conviction of the meaning of the stranger's face, which still flared for him like a smokey torch. It had not come to him, the knowledge, on the wings of experience; it had brushed him, jostled him, upset him, with the disrespect of chance, the insolence of an accident. Now that the illumination had begun, however, it blazed to the zenith, and what he presently stood there gazing at was the sounded void of his life. (Henry James, "The Beast in the Jungle")

(34) In Los Angeles paddling is being reintroduced in elementary and junior high schools after a five-year ban. Stringent guidelines say that only as a last resort, only with parental approval, only after a review of medical and disciplinary records, and only away from other kids may one to three swats be administered by a principal, assistant principal or administrative dean, with a staff witness. Students who absolutely refuse to be paddled must be offered a "reasonable alternative." ("What's Going on at School," *Changing Times*, September 1980)

(35) The man who opens for the first time a doorway into the future and who hears faint and far off, like surf on unknown reefs, the tumult and magnificence of an age beyond his own is confronted not alone with the scorn of his less perceptive fellows,

but even with the problem of finding the words to impose his vision upon contemporaries inclined to the belief that the world's time is short and its substance far sunk in decay. To achieve this well-nigh impossible task, Bacon had to take the language of his period and, like the seer he was, give old words new grandeur and significance, blow, in effect, a trumpet against time, darkness, and the failure of all things human. (Loren Eiseley, *The Man Who Saw Through Time*)

(36) The man of understanding can no more sit quiet and resigned while his country lets its literature decay, and lets good writing meet with contempt, than a good doctor could sit quiet and contented while some ignorant child was infecting itself with tuberculosis under the impression that it was merely eating jam tarts. (Ezra Pound, *A B C of Reading*)

V. Problem Pieces

(37) In order to be eligible for the independent project at Columbia this summer, you must be at least 18 years old, you must have completed the history requirement of the school, and you must pass an interview given by the faculty sponsors and students who participated in the program last summer. Perhaps the interview is the most crucial step in gaining admittance to the program. If for some reason the applicant is found unsuited to the program by those who know it best, he will not be accepted, no matter how qualified he may be in terms of teacher recommendations and academic success.

(38) Two questions remain, after much busy antiquarianism, concerning Leonardo's death — the question of the exact form of his religion, and the question whether Francis the First was present at the time. They are of about equally little importance in the estimate of Leonardo's genius. The directions in his will concerning the thirty masses and the great candles for the church of Saint Florentin are things of course, their real purpose being immediate and practical; and on no theory of religion could these hurried offices be of much consequence. We forget them in speculating how one who had been always so desirous of beauty, but desired it always in such precise and definite forms, as hands or flowers or hair, looked forward now into the vague land, and experienced the last curiosity. (Walter Pater, *The Renaissance*)

(39) *The Godfather* is a marvelous film. It is not a romantic vision of crime as some people complain, but a realistic view of a cruel but sometimes tender world. Marlon Brando is terrific in his part. I can believe that he was the Don because he reminds me of a wonderful old man I once knew who also did some bad things, he was finally arrested for embezzling, but he was often kind to the kids in our neighborhood and once took me to the amusement park across town.

(40) The early ideal of a city that it was a marketplace in which to exchange produce, and a mere trading-post for merchants, apparently still survives in our minds and is constantly reflected in our schools. We have either failed to realize that cities have become great centres of production and manufacture in which a huge population is engaged, or we have lacked sufficient presence of mind to adjust ourselves to the change. We admire much more the men who accumulate riches, and who gather to themselves the results of industry, than the men who actually carry forward industrial processes; and, as has been pointed out, our schools still prepare children almost exclusively for commercial and professional life. (Jane Addams, *Democracy and Social Ethics*)

(41) An ugly study in mob violence, unrelieved by any human grace save the futile reproach of a minority and some mild post-lynching remorse, is contained in "The Ox-Bow Incident," which was delivered to the Rivoli on Saturday by Twentieth Century-Fox in as brazen a gesture as any studio has ever indulged. For it is hard to imagine a picture with less promise commercially. In a little over an hour, it exhibits most of the baser shortcomings of men — cruelty, blood-lust, ruffianism, pusillanimity and sordid pride. It shows a tragic violation of justice with little backlash to sweeten the bitter draught. And it puts a popular actor, Henry Fonda, in a very dubious light. But it also points a moral, bluntly and unremittingly, to show the horror of mob rule. And it has the virtue of uncompromising truth. . . . (Bosley Crowther, *New York Times*, 10 May 1943)

(42) Frankly, that Mr. Thomas has not worked out in his capacity with you is surprising. He has strong recommendations. His last employer was disappointed to lose him and praised him for his alertness, imagination, and industry. In his interview, he admitted that his education had not been in the area of his keenest interest. Perhaps you remember that Mr. Thomas received a

B.A. in Economics. It was later in his career that he began to write. I have read several of his interviews with noted scientists (those that have appeared in *The Post*) and the charming children's book he published last fall. I must say that his writing seems quite professional.

We of the agency involved in his application are sorry that his scientific writing is "sub-standard." As you are aware, our firm takes pains to screen its applicants; we do not recommend an applicant if there seems to be any risk. Perhaps, then, this was one of those rare cases where . . .

(43) A tropical hurricane is a vast whirlwind that sweeps for days together over sea and land and is capable of doing a greater aggregate of damage than the tornado on account of the much larger area embraced in its path. It leaves ruin in its wake, yet stout buildings withstand its assaults and well-found ships plow safely through it. The entire life history of the tornado is usually compassed within less than an hour, and the path of destruction is seldom more than a quarter of a mile wide and some scores of miles long. At any one place along the path the whole thing is over in a minute. Within these narrow limits of space and time it does its deadly work with a thoroughness only rivaled by the deviltries of modern warfare. (C.F. Talman, *A Book About the Weather*)

(44) There were dramatic moments as I looked down on the floor — Charlie Halleck sitting alone, and Senator Strom Thurmond striding up to greet him, newly ensconced on the Republican side. John Tower, once more the lone Republican in the Texas delegation, bereft of his colleagues from Dallas and Midland. Somebody said, "Those Louisiana boys are sure taking over," speaking of Hale Boggs and Russell Long, who just won the Number Two place vacated by Humphrey, against the formidable opposition of John Pastore and Mike Monroney. This surprised me in view of Hale's vote on Civil Rights and Medicare and the Democratic Party's losing Louisiana. But everybody knows him as a fighter, and it's so easy to like him. (Lady Bird Johnson, *A White House Diary*)

(45) The consummate fatuousness of dialogue about compulsory class attendance threatens to exacerbate the already egregious dichotomy between the voluble, radical members of the school and the unctuous, obsequious minions of the pedagogues. Hyper-

bolic polarization of sentiments is the infallible consequence of extended, circumlocutious debate emanating from nescience. A rational but expeditious compromise augurs to be the singular solution to terminate the metaphorical psychomachy that this institution is suffering. This newspaper exhorts its student readership to commence equilateral concessions.

(46) Polar bears live at the North Pole. They eat fish which they catch when they put their paws through the ice. They are huge animals who require 20 or more pounds of fish a day. They have white fur which matches the snow of the Polar Region. They are well camouflaged wherever they go. Their main occupation is catching fish and protecting their cubs, which are born black and turn white later.

(47) The metric system is quite an interesting topic. I feel that it will take a long while till the United States adopts this system. The system seems to be working almost all over the world except in the U.S. The people of the United States, especially the teachers and students, might find it hard but will eventually understand it. However, those people in other countries don't seem to have many problems. The older generation in the U.S. would probably hate this system but after a while they will see how easily this system works because of the simple arithmetic done.

(48) Stories of hauntings are reported under so many different specific conditions that no single illustration can be typical of very many. But they usually are similar in that they seem wierd, "scary," hair-raising. This, of course, is largely because, as reported, they are mysterious and seem to be contrary to all known explanations. It must be remembered that this result follows necessarily because the idea began without the knowledge of psi ability, and when even simple signs of it, like cases of ESP, were often considered supernatural. And also, both long ago and even today, they are experienced by people who still, not far beneath the surface so to speak, believed in or were ready to believe in the idea of spirits, invisible entities with intelligence of their own who can affect human beings. (Louisa E. Rhine, *PSI What Is It? The Story of ESP and PK)*

VIII.
Assignments for the Photographs

A. *New City, New York,* 1971 (p. 2) Arno Rafael Minkkinen

1. Create a sentence that is literal about the picture. Create a second sentence that uses figurative language to enlarge the first.

2. For what might the tree, the feet, and the sky be metaphors?

3. Paragraph: Write an example paragraph that begins with one of these options:

   A. "In my mind I have always swung from trees."
   B. "Sometimes lying on the ground looking up through trees. . ."
   C. "I think we have got it all wrong."

4. Paragraph: Use the situation of or feeling in this picture as an analogy to something else.

B. *Untitled,* 1977 (p. 4) Ann Mandelbaum

1. Create a metaphor or simile for the white table
                              the footstones
                              the leaves
                              the dark hedge

2. In a sentence describe the relationship between the objects and the child in the picture, and the dominant expanse of grass.

3. Outline: Create an outline for a composition about one of your childhood memories. Make sure that your topic sentences prove your thesis statement. Identify the methods of paragraph development you intend to use.

4. Paragraph: Define nostalgia or sentimentality and then determine if this picture is nostalgic or sentimental.

C. *New York City,* 1963 (p. 10) Lee Friedlander

1. Discuss in a paragraph the differences in emphasis and syntax in these two statements:

   The car is fenced off from us, carefully locked beyond our reach; the wire fence is impenetrable.

   It is a strange sight, that car pent up behind all of that glistening wire; all last summer the car lay there like a sullen, caged animal.

2. Paragraph: Describe something that was once locked off from you, that you wished desperately or mischievously to touch, taste, or behold.

3. Composition: Take some stand about the current consciousness of security — personal and property. (You may want to use a cause and effect paragraph.)

D. *Terra Firma*, 1974 (p. 15) Bobbi Carrey

In making this picture, the photographer combined two images: one of a rural landscape and another of herself with arms upraised.

1. Create two statements of response to the picture. In the first, speak for yourself; in the second, for someone of the opposite sex about your age. Both statements should be cast in the first person.

2. Paragraph: Using the shuttle method, compare the look and feel (tonalties and texture) of this picture to those of any other picture in this book.

3. Composition: Discuss the larger issues provoked by this picture. What kind or kinds of statement does it make about ecology, productivity, mankind, nature?

E. *Newark, New Jersey*, 1962 (p. 18) Lee Friedlander

1. Create sentences from details in this picture by employing the following forms:
   a. Simple sentence
   b. Inversion
   c. Antithesis
   d. Periodic sentence
   e. Compound sentence
   f. Compound-complex sentence
   g. Complex sentence

2. Paragraph: Make a list of the significant details in this picture. Then decide what the two figures are watching, create a topic sentence, and write the paragraph.

3. Paragraph: Place yourself in a lunchroom, bus station, movie lounge, or another location and observe carefully a stranger. Create a descriptive sketch of this person. Try to use connotative details.

F. *Untitled* (p. 20) Anthony Barboza

1. Create three sentences describing some element of this picture. If possible, use metaphor and simile. In one of the sentences, describe the sounds made by the cart and men.

2. Paragraph: Describe an arduous chore that is worth doing.

3. Composition: Describe an incident that happened to you in a foreign city or in a place you had never before visited. This incident could have taken place upon your first visit to a distant relative.

G. *Untitled* (p. 32) Anthony Barboza

1. Paragraph: Assume that you were on hand when these teenagers posed for the picture. Describe what occurred, but limit yourself to only one spoken comment by either of the teenagers or by the photographer.

2. Dialogue: Invent a dialogue between these two people or two others about a picture in which they appear.

3. Paragraph: Describe this picture for someone who has not seen it. End your paragraph by determining the significance of the placement of the girl's hands.

4. Composition: Describe your relationship with a close friend — someone to whom you are not amorously attached.

H. *The Bikeriders* (p. 37) Danny Lyon

1. Alter the emphasis of these sentences:

   The bikerider paused for the camera; his face was mud-spattered and seemingly pained, but he was delighted with himself — he had finished ahead of his friendly rival.

   The bikerider idled up to the photographer; he raised his proud and muddy face for a quick portrait.

   After idling up to the photographer, the bikerider smiled, for although the race had been treacherous, he had finished better than he had expected to.

2. Paragraph: Discuss the significance of the details in the background of this picture.

3. Composition: Photographers have styles as writers have prose styles. Attempt to compare the style of this picture with one by Richards or Barboza. (Note the uses of light, shadow, words within the picture, and placement of key details.)

I. *Papa, Squam Lake - II*, 1973 (p. 48) Kelly Wise

The old gentlemen was engaged in what turned out to be his last swim when the photographer took this picture. It was a sweltering August day. He was helped down to the lake and into the water by his family. Once there, he swam a short distance with gentle vigor.

1. In a paragraph compare these two sentences:

   The old man stepped gingerly into the water; he emitted a soft whistle as the lake ran its chill but soothing fingers up his limbs.

Stepping gingerly into the water, the old man emitted a soft whistle; the lake was chill but also very soothing.

2. Complete the statement by using a metaphor or personification:

   In those outstretched arms . . .

3. Paragraph: In a chronological or spatial paragraph describe the old man's odyssey down to the water.

4. Composition: Using the block form, compare the statement made by this picture with that made by Wise's LOTTE JACOBI (p. 110).

5. Composition: In the first person describe your efforts to help an older person understand or do something.

J. *Untitled* (p. 51) Eugene Richards

1. On the left of a sheet of paper, make a list of the important details in this picture. To the right, assign a mood or emotion to each of these details. In a sentence, describe their overall effect.

2. Paragraph: Using spatial organization, describe the exterior of the house and the feelings it provokes.

3. Composition: Invent a personage who is living in this house. Describe her or his day, the responses to the world outside the house, the reasons for the bare clothesline and the sign in the window.

4. Composition: Discuss the use of presence of shadows in any two of Eugene Richards' pictures in this book.

K. *Untitled*, 1972 (p. 61) Steve Wicks

1. Create a sentence that literally describes the relationship of the circus man to the elephant; then create a sentence that uses figurative language to describe the relationship of the elephant to the circus man.

2. Paragraph: Choose an act or a creature from a circus or carnival and describe from a child's perspective the impression it makes. Use third person.

3. Composition: Compare and contrast this picture with Arno Minkkinen's picture of the feet and the tree. (p. 2) Comment upon the placement of key details and the uses of the background in these pictures.

L. *Untitled*, 1979 (p. 66) Ann Mandelbaum

1. Make a list of nouns that could possibly describe what the boy feels when that finger is thrust into his back. Cast those nouns in phrases of simile and metaphor.

2. In a sentence create a personification for the fence.

3. Create three different sentences to explain why the boy is standing at the fence, gazing across that road.

4. Paragraph: Write a paragraph (in the first person) about the fence, the boy, and the finger.

5. Paragraph: Write a paragraph (in the third person) about a teenager who is followed and accosted by a stranger.

M. *Untitled* (p. 70) Eugene Richards

1. Create sentences that relate to the picture by employing the following openings:

   Gerund   Infinitive   Adverbial clause   Preposition (of or with)

2. Composition: Describe the buildup to the conflict of the picture and invent a dialogue that resolves that conflict. (You will want to decide if the girl is going to her first communion, a wedding, or a costume party.) Employ at least one paragraph of chronological organization.

3. Composition: Certain streets, city blocks, and stores have a special atmosphere. Describe a street, city block, or store that you believe is unusual.

N. *Golden Horde,* 1974 (p. 74) Cary Wasserman

For this picture, the photographer used a very slow shutter speed so that he could suggest the on-the-spot demolition of the Golden Horde Restaurant. Time is not frozen in this photograph as it is in most photographs.

1. Make a list of the significant details in the picture and create a topic sentence for a paragraph about the demolition of the Golden Horde Restaurant.

2. Paragraph: Describe the effect of the words (some in crisp focus, some in blur) in this picture.

3. Composition: Write about something in the process of deterioration. (One of your paragraphs may be a cause and effect paragraph, another a chronological paragraph.)

O. *Swing,* 1972 (p. 81) Kelly Wise

1. For each of the following details in the picture create a figurative phrase:

   the dog   the swing
   the branches overhead   the wispy fog
   the patch of ice

2. Paragraph: Assume that you were with the photographer when this picture was taken. Create a mood paragraph by describing the sounds, the smells, the touch of the cold and the fog upon your skin that the picture necessarily omits.

3. Composition: Discuss the relation of the dog and the swing.

4. Composition: Compare and contrast this photograph with either Carrey's TERRA FIRMA (p. 15) or Wasserman's EMBUDO PASS, NEW MEXICO. (p. 105) Use block method.

P. *Mr. and Mrs. Steve Mills, Pilgrim Theatre,* 1974 (p. 87) Roswell Angier

1. Create a simile and a metonymy for the locked hands in this picture.

2. In separate sentences, describe how you think each person feels about posing for this portrait.

3. Paragraph: Create a paragraph about two other people who form a congenial but unlikely couple.

4. Dialogue: That the oldest living vaudevillian actor and his young wife would pose for their portrait in this way suggests something about their lives together. Create a convincing dialogue between these two people or for two other people who are older than you. Try to seal the dialogue with a concluding and provocative statement or retort.

Q. *Untitled,* 1977 (p. 92) Starr Ockenga

1. Create a compound sentence describing the relationship between these two children. Create a second sentence that employs figurative language to enlarge the first. Create a third sentence in which the emphasis is placed upon the puppeteer.

2. Paragraph: Create an analogy paragraph using the idea of a puppet and puppeteer.

3. Composition: Discuss the ways two photographers pose their subjects by comparing two of the pictures in this book. Place one of your topic sentences at the end of a paragraph. As methods of paragraph development, use example and comparison or contrast.

4. Composition: An old cliché is that children are cruel. From your experience, attack or defend that statement. Define the nature of cruelty in some childplay. Attempt to explain why children sometimes submit to cruel games.

R. *Untitled* (p. 98) **Eugene Richards**

1. Using details from the picture, create sentences which employ figurative language:

    the horse's hooves (metonymy)
    the padlock (personification)
    the mechanical ride (simile)
    the baby smiling in the poster (metaphor)

2. Paragraph: Write a paragraph in which the topic sentence, appearing at the very end, asserts in your own words that in essence we all partake of substitute thrills when we lack the opportunity to experience the real thrill (in this case actually riding a horse).

3. Composition: Argue for the necessity of certain escapes, secret or otherwise (golf, terrifying movies, situation comedies), in order to minimize the pressures of school work or a strenuous job. The opening paragraph should assert your thesis; the other paragraphs should offer convincing examples to support his thesis.

S. *Embudo Pass, New Mexico,* 1974 (p. 105) **Cary Wasserman**

1. Make a list of the objects in the picture; assume that you were going to write about the arrangement of those objects, and, therefore, list the transitions you would employ to relate and distinguish them.

2. Create a sentence about the chair hanging from the wall. Expand or reduce that sentence to change the emphasis.

3. Paragraph: Using spatial organization for your paragraph, describe this picture in detail.

4. Composition: Describe the process and art of collecting something. (One of your paragraphs may be classification and division and/or process.)

T. *Lotte Jacobi,* 1978 (p. 110) **Kelly Wise**

1. In a paragraph explain how these two statements differ:

    Pretense is an important factor in this picture; we realize that the old woman posing for the photograph is in fact only pretending to be lost in thought.

    The old woman in this picture is pretending to be lost in thought, a fact we as viewers easily recognize.

2. Complete these partial statements:

    Her skin was as delicate as _____
    A recollection, forgotten all these years, _____
    Lightly, her fingers touched her lips, as if _____

3. Composition: Invent a persona for this old woman and write a first-person monologue for her. Assume that she has just completed some activity dear to her — tending bees, crocheting a scarf, making wild blueberry jam — and now has indulged herself in a moment of revery. The first paragraph should describe the activity; the second her thoughts.

U. *Stairway,* 1972 (p. 117) Kelly Wise

1. Create a compound-complex sentence about the doll in this picture. (Assume that the child placed the doll and sock on the stairs.)

2. Create a complex sentence with a simile about the blurry form of the child.

3. Paragraph: We all remember certain frights of childhood, ones that seem less scary now that we are older. Write a paragraph about a fright you recall from your childhood.

4. Paragraph: Discuss the uses of light, shadow, and blur in this picture. Comment upon the effect of the glowing light at the top of the stairs.

V. *Andover, Massachusetts,* 1979 (p. 140)
Arno Rafael Minkkinen

1. Create two sentences about this picture — one employing antithesis, the other employing a balanced sentence.

2. Paragraph: Large and small, strong and tender, wisdom and innocence — these dichotomies are familiar in our everyday lives. Write a paragraph of contrast about the two figures in this picture. Use the shuttle method.

3. Composition: Describe some aspect of your relationship with a parent, grandparent, or close adult friend.

W. *Untitled* (p. 150) Anthony Barboza

1. In a single sentence, make a statement about the following elements of the picture:

   The flag
   The child
   The house

2. Paragraph: The American flag is a patriotic symbol that people use and respect in differing ways. Write a paragraph about a particular use of the American flag.

3. Paragraph: Write a paragraph about the child and the flag in this picture. Place your topic sentence at the end of the paragraph.

X. *Untitled* (p. 162) Anthony Barboza

1. In what ways would this scene strike various people? Write a sentence each from the point of view of the following:

   > A cabdriver who often parks opposite the wall
   > The girlfriend of Lupe
   > "Sneak"

2. Paragraph: Although the picture is black and white, the actual scene had many colors. Describe the scene as it might appear in color.

3. Composition: Write a composition (titled "Graffiti") about people who create graffiti or about a location in which you find graffiti. You may want to determine what lies behind the impulse to inscribe doors, walls, signs with words and drawings.

4. Composition: In either the first or the third person write a short narrative about someone who creates graffiti.

Y. *Boston Garden*, 1976 (p. 166) John A. Rizzo

1. Using details from this sports scene, create sentences with the following patterns:
   a. Antithesis
   b. Compound-complex
   c. That construction
   d. Gerund opener
   e. Inversion
   f. Infinitive opener
   g. Complex
   h. Balanced sentence, using phrases

2. Paragraph: Describe this scene from the point of view of a spectator in the front row. Use chronological and spatial organization. Include vivid details.

3. Composition: It is an amusing and sometimes instructive fact that we accept the artificial as real or depend upon the artificial to enrich the real. Why we do this is not easily explained. For instance, some of us may find professional wrestling more exciting and bloodcurdling than a fierce prizefight. In horror or mystery films, we may accept the most bogus coincidences and props and perhaps never scoff at the music that swells and orchestrates our emotional responses. Write a composition about some relation of the artificial to the real.

Z. *Untitled,* 1977 (p. 173) **Starr Ockenga**

1. Create a sentence about this picture in which you use personification and another in which you use metonymy.

2. Paragraph: These two children wear masks, make-up, head gear to act out a fantasy of their devising. The photographer arranged to meet them at a certain time one day, and they were given the opportunity to appear dressed in any way they wished. In a paragraph determine what they intend by their dress and pose. (Why is one head seemingly carried by the arm of the other child? Is there any significance to the inclusion of the rope in the picture?)

3. Composition: Define fantasy and write about a recurring fantasy that you or a friend have.

IX.
Bibliography

Adams, Henry. *The Education of Henry Adams.* Boston and New York: Houghton Mifflin, 1918.

Addams, Jane. *Democracy and Social Ethics.* New York: Macmillan, 1902.

Allen, Frederick Lewis. *Only Yesterday.* New York: Harper & Brothers, 1931.

Arnold, Grant. *Creative Lithography.* New York: Harper & Brothers, 1941.

Baldwin, James. *Go Tell It on the Mountain.* New York: Grosset and Dunlap, Inc., 1952, 1953.

Barth, John, *The Floating Opera.* 1956. Rev. edn. 1967, rep. New York: Bantam Books, 1972.

Bessy, Maurice. *A Pictorial History of Magic and the Supernatural.* London: Spring Books, 1964.

Blakeslee, Douglas, ed. *The Radio Amateur's Handbook 1973.* Newington, Conn.: American Radio Relay League, 1973.

Boyd, Ernest. "Aesthete: Model 1924." In *Fitzgerald and the Jazz Age.* Ed. M. and R. Crowley. New York: Charles Scribner's Sons, 1966.

Bradley, A.C. *Shakespearean Tragedy.* London: Macmillan and Co., Ltd., 1904, 1950.

Brooks, Charles S. *Chimney-Pot Papers.* New Haven: Yale Univ. Press, 1919.

Burke, Edmund. *Reflections on the Revolution in France.* 1790, 1793. Rpt. London: Dent (Everyman's Library). Ed. A.J. Grieve, 1910, 1964.

Cremin, Lawrence A. *The Transformation of the School.* New York: Vintage Books, 1961.

Crowther, Bosley. Review of "The Ox-Bow Incident." *The New York Times,* 10 May 1943.

Davis, Stephen. "Fela's Afro-Beat Revolt." *Saturday Review,* 22 July 1978.

Dreiser, Theodore. *Sister Carrie.* New York: Boni & Liveright, Inc., 1917.

Dubois, W.E.B. *John Brown.* Philadelphia: George W. Jacobs & Co., 1909.

Eble, Kenneth. *A Perfect Education.* New York: Macmillan Co., 1966.

Eiseley, Loren. *The Man Who Saw Through Time.* New York: Charles Scribner's Sons, 1961.

Emerson, Ralph Waldo. "Self-Reliance." *Essays* (First Series). 1841. Rpt. in *The Complete Essays and Other Writings of Ralph Waldo Emerson.* Ed. Brooks Atkinson. New York: Random House (Modern Library), 1950.

Emerson, Ralph Waldo. "The Times." *English Traits.* 1856. Rpt. in *The Complete Essays and Other Writings of Ralph Waldo Emerson.* Ed. Brooks Atkinson. New York: Random House (Modern Library), 1950.

Encyclopaedia Britannica. 11th edn. Cambridge: Cambridge Univ. Press, 1910-11.

Evans, G. Heberton, III and Robert E. Anderson. *Lacrosse Fundamentals.* New York: A.S. Barnes and Co., Inc., 1966.

Fitzgerald, F. Scott. *The Great Gatsby.* New York: Charles Scribner's Sons, 1925.

Foy, Adele. "Cog without a Wheel." *The New York Times,* Monday, 21 July 1980.

Gardner, Howard. "Gifted Wordmakers." *Psychology Today,* September 1980.

Garland, Hamlin, *A Son of the Middle Border.* New York: The Macmillan Co., 1917.

Goldman, Emma. "What I Believe." *The New York World.* 1908. Reprinted in *Red Emma Speaks: Writings and Speeches by Emma Goldman.* Ed. Alix Kates Shulman. New York: Random House, 1972.

Grahame, Kenneth. *The Wind in the Willows.* New York: Charles Scribner's Sons, 1908.

Harrison, Jane. *Prolegomena to the Study of Greek Religion.* Cambridge: Cambridge Univ. Press, 1903.

Haskins, Jim. *James Van DerZee: The Picture Takin' Man.* New York: Dodd, Mead & Co., Inc., 1979.

Herzberg, Robert J. *So You Want To Be a Ham.* Indianapolis: Howard W. Sams, 1965.

Hughes, Robert. "A Haunted Man." TIME Magazine, 31 July 1972.

Hughes, Rosemary. "Joseph Haydn." *Chamber Music.* Ed. Alec Robertson. Harmondsworth: Penguin Books, 1957.

Irving, Washington. "John Bull." *The Sketch Book*. New York: G.P. Putnam; Hurd and Houghton, 1866.

James, Henry. *The Novels and Tales of Henry James*. New York: Charles Scribner's Sons, 1922.

James, William. *Talks to Teachers on Psychology and to Students on Some of Life's Ideals*. New York: Henry Holt & Co., 1907.

Johnson, Lady Bird. *A White House Diary*. New York: Holt, Rinehart and Winston, 1970.

Johnson, Samuel. "Life of Richard Savage." 1744. Rep. in *Lives of the English Poets*. 2 vols. London: Oxford Univ. Press (World's Classics), 1952.

Joyce, James. "The Dead." *Dubliners*. New York: B.W. Huebsch, 1916.

Keller, Helen. "Three Days to See." In *Adventures in Contentment*. Ed. David Grayson. New York: Doubleday, 1907.

Kimball, John. *Biology*. Third ed. Reading, Mass.: Addison Wesley, 1974.

Leonard, John. "Books of the Times." *The New York Times*, Monday, 21 July 1980.

Mabie, Hamilton Wright. "Theocritus on Cape Cod." *The Oxford Book of American Essays*. Ed. Brander Matthews. New York: Oxford Univ. Press, 1914.

Macaulay, Thomas Babington. *The History of England from the Accession of James II*. 1849-1861. Rpt. in *The Works of Lord Macaulay*. Ed. Lady Trevelyan for the Jenson Society. (N.p.) 1907.

Mack, Maynard. "The World of *Hamlet*." *The Yale Review*, XLI (1952), pp. 502-23.

Mailer, Norman. *The Armies of the Night*. New York: The New American Library, 1968.

Mariani, John. "Out-of-Sight-Seeing." *Saturday Review*, 22 July 1978.

May, Rollo. *The Courage to Create*. New York: W.W. Norton & Co., Inc., 1975.

McCarthy, Mary. *Memories of a Catholic Girlhood*. New York: Harcourt, Brace and Co., 1957.

Melville, Herman. *Moby Dick*. 1851. Rpt. New York: W.W. Norton and Co., Inc. Ed. Harrison Hayford and Hershel Parker, 1967.

Moore, Gaylen. "Lotte Jacobi: Born with a Photographer's Eye." *The New York Times Magazine,* 16 September 1979.

Nabokov, Vladimir. *Speak, Memory.* New York: G.P. Putnam's Sons, 1966.

Newman, John Henry (Cardinal). *The Idea of a University Defined and Illustrated.* London: Longmans, Green and Co., 1912.

Nin, Anais. *The Diary of Anais Nin, Volume 3, 1939-1944.* Ed. Gunther Stuhlmann. New York: Harcourt Brace Jovanovich, 1969.

Pater, Walter. *The Renaissance; Studies in Art and Poetry.* Rev. and enl. London and New York: Macmillan and Co., 1888. Orig. ed. 1873.

Plumb, J.H. *The First Four Georges.* London: B.H. Batsford, Ltd., 1956.

Poe, Edgar Allan. "The Fall of the House of Usher." *The Works of Edgar Allan Poe.* New York: Scribner's, 1902.

Pope, Alexander. "Epigram. Engraved on the Collar of a Dog which I gave to his Royal Highness." *The Poems of Alexander Pope* (one-volume edition of the Twickenham Text). Ed. John Butt. London: Methuen & Co., Ltd., 1963.

Porter, Katherine Anne. *Ship of Fools.* Boston: Atlantic Little, Brown, 1962.

Pound, Ezra. *A B C of Reading.* New York: New Directions. No date. Original copyright 1934; New Haven: Yale Univ. Press.

Rhine, Louisa E. *PSI What Is It? The Story of ESP and PK.* New York: Harper & Row, Publishers, 1975.

Russell, Bill and Taylor Branch. "The Highs of the Game." *The New York Times Magazine,* 16 September 1979.

"Russification" (editorial). *The New York Times,* 6 July 1972.

Sinclair, Upton. *The Jungle.* New York: Viking, 1905, 1946.

Spock, Benjamin. *Baby and Child Care.* Rev. ed. New York: Pocket Books, Inc., 1968.

Steinbeck, John. *The Grapes of Wrath.* New York: Random House (The Modern Library), 1939.

Steiner, George. *The Death of Tragedy.* New York: Alfred Knopf, 1961.

Strayer, Joseph R. *Western Europe in the Middle Ages.* New York: Appleton-Century-Crofts, 1955.

"The Talk of the Town" (obituary of Paul Desmond). *The New Yorker*, 20 June 1977, p. 25.

Talman, Charles Fitzhugh. *A Book About the Weather*. New York: Blue Ribbon Books, Inc., 1931.

Thackeray, William Makepeace. *Vanity Fair*. 1848, 1864. Rpt. New York: Random House (Modern Library). Ed. Joseph Warren Beach, 1950.

Thoreau, Henry David. *The Journal of Henry D. Thoreau*. Boston: Houghton Mifflin, 1906.

Thoreau, Henry David. *Walden*. 1854. Rpt. in *The Portable Thoreau*. Ed. Carl Bode. New York: Viking, 1947.

Toomer, Jean. *Cane*. New York: Liveright Publishing Corp. 1923, 1951.

Torres, Jose. *Sting Like a Bee*. New York: Curtis Books, 1971.

Tuchman, Barbara W. *A Distant Mirror: The Calamitous 14th Century*. New York: Alfred A. Knopf, 1978.

Twain, Mark (Samuel Clemens). *Life on the Mississippi*. 1883. Rpt. New York: Signet Books, 1961.

Twain, Mark (Samuel Clemens). "The £1,000,000 Bank-Note." *The Complete Short Stores of Mark Twain*. Ed. Charles Neider. Garden City: Doubleday, 1957.

Updike, John. "Upright Carpentry." *Assorted Prose*. New York: Alfred Knopf, 1965. (Originally in *The New Yorker* magazine, 10 May 1958.)

Veronis, John J. "Profitable Partnership: Business and the Arts." *Saturday Review of the Arts*, 1, 4, (7 April 1973).

Wharton, Edith. *The House of Mirth*. 1905. Rpt. New York: Bantam Books, 1962.

"What's Going on at School." *Changing Times*, September 1980.

Whitman, Walt. "Preface to *Leaves of Grass*." *The Oxford Book of American Essays*. Ed. Brander Matthews. New York: Oxford Univ. Press, 1914.

Wicker, Tom. *A Time to Die*. New York: Quadrangle/The New York Times Book Co., 1975.

Wilson, C.L. and W.E. Loomis, *Botany*. 3rd ed. New York: Holt, Rinehart and Winston, 1962.

Wolfe, Tom. *The Kandy-Kolored Tangerine-Flake Streamline Baby*. New York: Farrar, Straus & Giroux, 1965.

Index

203